YOUNG PERSON'S GUIDE
TO OPERA

By the same Author

IMMORTAL HOUR: THE LIFE AND PERIOD
OF RUTLAND BOUGHTON

YOUNG PERSON'S GUIDE TO CONCERTS

Young Person's Guide to *Guide to* OPERA

by
MICHAEL HURD

ROY PUBLISHERS, INC.
NEW YORK 10021

First published in U.S.A., 1965
by Roy Publishers, Inc.
30 East 74th Street
New York

© *Michael Hurd 1963*
Reprinted 1968

Library of Congress Catalog No. 66-11511

Printed in Great Britain

Contents

Preface

LIKE its companion, the *Young Person's Guide to Concerts*, this book is intended primarily for young people, but I hope it may also prove useful to older and more experienced opera-goers who find themselves in need of a brief guide to the main facts behind opera and the opera house.

I record, with great pleasure, my gratitude to Miss Anna Pollak and Sir David Webster, the General Administrator of the Royal Opera House, Covent Garden, for their patience in answering the numerous questions with which I bombarded them. Such errors as may have crept into the following chapters should not be attributed to them.

MICHAEL HURD

West Liss,
Hampshire,
May 1963.

PART ONE
The Ingredients of Opera

I

The Conventions of Opera

'OPERA,' thundered Dr. Johnson, in a fine frenzy of disapproval, 'is an exotic and irrational entertainment.'

Had he been a little less positive, admitting that the opera he spoke of, the opera of the eighteenth century, was only *apparently* irrational, then it might have been possible to agree with him. For opera is indeed exotic and, looked at without sympathy and understanding, does appear irrational—irrational, at least, by the standards of the average Englishman.

The trouble is that this Englishman has been brought up without the benefit of a strong national operatic tradition and therefore thinks of opera as one of the luxuries his country imports from abroad. Moreover, he has few opportunities to taste this luxury for himself. If he lives in London he can enjoy fine performances at Covent Garden and Sadler's Wells almost any day of the week; but if he lives elsewhere his opportunities are scant indeed. An occasional visit from the London opera houses when they are on tour—this is as much as he can expect to hear of first-class opera on his own doorstep. For the rest he must depend on records, radio and television, and the odd performance of tired operatic warhorses by worthy, but hopelessly inadequate, local amateurs.

How different the position is for an Italian or a German, or even a Frenchman! Each town of any size in Italy and Germany supports its own Opera House, as its English equivalent supports a Football Club. Perhaps they do not always reach the highest standards, but at least these local opera houses exist, and this simple fact assures a strong and healthy operatic tradition. France, certainly, is less enthusiastic, but, even so, comes nowhere near our own country for operatic indifference. Is it then surprising that Dr. Johnson's harsh description still rings bells of truth in English ears?

In earlier days it may have been quite proper to regard with suspicion the things in which other countries delighted, but experience has made us less confident that our own standards are unquestionable. And although many Englishmen still find time to dismiss opera as being ridiculous and fit only for the unaccountable foreigner, increasing numbers are happy to accept it on its own terms—and these are the only terms which can ever lead to an understanding and enjoyment of its subtleties.

The point about opera is that it is cast in a particular convention. It is not drama, in the ordinary sense; nor is it a concert of music. Opera is something special and entirely of its own kind. Our job, as intelligent listeners, is to discover what its nature really is, not complain that it isn't what we think it *ought* to be. No one in England is dismayed by the rules of cricket. We accept the peculiar conventions and proceed to enjoy the game on its own terms. We do not complain that its place is infinitely slower than that of football—we adjust our scale of time-values and sit out the warm summer afternoons, perfectly content that

4

cricket has its own speed and thus its own sort of thrills. And so it should be with opera.

At the root of operatic convention is the fact that music can heighten the expression of emotion. Music works upon our imagination. Through its magic we seem to feel things as acutely as we do in real life, for music touches our memory of past emotions, reawakening them so that they seem to live again. And in opera the feelings that music arouses are made more real by their association with words and drama. Within certain limits orchestral music can be interpreted by the listener in any way he chooses. But with opera there is no such conflict: the words and the dramatic action tell us what we are to feel and the music tells us how we are to feel it.

Yet it is upon this rock that so many people founder. Words and music can arouse such vivid emotions that the actual manner in which they are being presented may suddenly seem artificial and foolish. Thus, in the middle of a death-bed scene, where we are moved to tears by the music and the dramatic situation, the dying heroine may be called upon to sing at the top of her powerful voice. This, we tell ourselves, is not how death-bed scenes are conducted in real life—opera is therefore a cheat and a fraud. But the fault is with us: we have accepted as truth the powerful illusion that can be spun from words and music, and have then gone on to judge this illusion by standards of reality that do not apply to it.

In opera we must accept that the singing voice not only takes over the rôle of the speaking voice, but is at the same time an instrument through which emotion is conveyed in musical terms. If we find this convention intolerable then we had better leave opera alone once and for all. But, as conventions go, it is no more unreasonable than those we

5

swallow every day. Films and television play tricks with time and space that have no parallel in everyday experience. Shakespeare's characters speak in fluent blank verse, and no one is surprised. Art, in fact, can only express itself by means of a convention—the convention is simply the form in which the message is written.

Opera, however, presents unusual difficulties to anyone who enjoys the ordinary theatre but is not accustomed to the peculiarities of music. To begin with, words and music do not move at the same pace. A musical phrase may need a certain length of time to complete itself, but the words it is expressing may be used up long before this happens. Either the words must be repeated, or drawn out over several notes. Whichever solution the composer adopts the result is unreal *as speech*. But if we adjust our minds to the fact that it is not speech, and was never intended to be speech, then the problem vanishes.

On the other hand music can often explain in a moment something that it would take many words to make clear. Here it is the librettist (the man who writes the words (libretto) of an opera) who must be on his guard and avoid treading on the composer's special ground. Bearing these problems in mind composer and librettist will work out that extraordinary compromise between words and music that makes up the special art of opera. For that is what opera is: an art of compromise. And its main ingredients— the Aria and the Recitative—are a direct outcome of this principle.

The earliest operas tended to emphasize the words at the expense of the music and thus consisted mainly of *Recitative*—that is to say: musical speech. The result was horribly dull. But gradually music began to assert itself. At points where the words expressed emotion the early opera composers so far forgot themselves as to let their music blossom into something very like a song. Soon they had expanded these emotional boiling-points into regular tunes, or *Arias*, and within a very short time a workable convention was born.

This convention was based on a simple observation of the nature of drama. Since the pattern of any story moves in a series of steps, wherein action brings about a situation which leads, in turn, to further action and fresh situations, what more natural than to exploit this in musical terms? Action, in a play, is made clear by speech. The musical equivalent of speech is Recitative. Actions lead to Situations—that is to say, the moment when the characters in a play realize that something has happened and react accordingly. This, of course, is also the moment when emotions are released and thus can best be expressed in musical terms by the Aria, which simply translates the emotions into the flowing lines of melody.

Thus, there is in opera a continuous ebb and flow between action and emotion, between swift-moving recitative and reflective aria. At one moment it is the words that are important—at the next, the music has its way. The convention allows each to make its contribution as effectively as possible.

At different times in the history of opera this basic convention has been interpreted in different ways. In the early part of the eighteenth century the fashion was for opera to be extremely formal. Recitative and aria remained in watertight compartments, each performing its special function. The dramatic side of these operas thus moved forward in a series of jerks, while, from a musical point of view, they are often little more than a concert of arias, linked together by dull recitatives. Moreover, the arias

The Ingredients of Opera

themselves were squeezed into a standard three-part pattern (two main statements of a tune, separated by a contrasting middle section), and it was generally held that no aria might express more than one emotion at a time. In this way the drama remained frozen throughout each aria and only moved forward again with the next recitative— the effect is rather that of a film which every now and again stops moving and becomes a still photograph. Artificial as this method now seems it was perfectly logical in an age that exalted the singer above everything else in opera. The early eighteenth-century audience did not go to the opera house for realistic drama, but for fine singing, and their operas were planned accordingly. In spite of this it must not be forgotten that in the hands of a great genius like Handel even these limited procedures turn into something that still has power over a present-day audience.

During the second half of the eighteenth century, however, fashions changed and though the singer remained important the needs of dramatic truth began to be recognized. In consequence the conventions governing aria and recitative became less rigid. In the operas of Gluck and Mozart we find arias that do not hold up the action—the characters sing, but the drama develops as a result of what they are singing. Opera, in other words, became more human and realistic.

In varying degrees this trend continued throughout the nineteenth century. Gradually the barriers between aria and recitative were blurred over in favour of a continuous flow of music which might vary in pace and emotion according to the needs of the drama. We see this sort of development most clearly in the operas of Verdi: in his later works it is still obvious whether, at any given moment, we are listening to something that is more aria than recita-

8

tive, but we shall be hard pressed to find a division between the two.

Wagner, on the other hand, aiming at a rather different sort of opera, made a clean sweep of the older operatic conventions and substituted a continuous orchestral background which unfolds like a symphony. Against this the voices sing a melodious recitative. The business of revealing emotion is now given entirely to the orchestra, and the voices often seem little more than extra instruments which happen to have words attached to them. However, the method suits the stories that Wagner chose for his Music Dramas, for these are less concerned with physical action than with the inner development of character and emotion and the orchestra is able to reveal this development regardless of the action on the stage.

Modern interpretation of the basic operatic conventions has tended to make use of a wide variety of procedures without emphasizing any one in particular. The modern composer simply uses any technique that seems appropriate to the situation. In general, however, the distinction between aria and recitative can still be seen—though the outlines may be 'blurred over'. A composer will allow the emotions of his characters to boil over in lyrical phrases of great melodic beauty, but will avoid forcing them into the straitjacket of a self-contained aria. He will use the orchestra as a means of commenting upon the action as well as a means of supporting the voice. Modern opera aims at dramatic realism, but allows a degree of musical stylization.

Certain other features of opera are sometimes referred to as 'conventions', but they are, in fact, no more than artistic fashions. If you go to hear an eighteenth-century opera you must, besides the purely musical conventions, expect to put up with stories in which dire tragedies are suddenly averted by the intervention of some god or other descending in a chariot of fire. Skip forward a hundred years and the opera will deal with pure heroines and noble heroes, wicked villains who dabble in the supernatural, last-minute rescues and spectacular crowd scenes. Another hundred years and the stage is groaning with tales of passion in sordid back streets. Opera has always reflected the literary and dramatic tastes of the period—even trivial, passing fashions (like the sudden craze for Japanese things that prompted Puccini to write *Madame Butterfly*) leave their mark. But we should no more complain about this aspect of opera than we should about any other change of taste. Our duty as sensible listeners is to accept such things for what they are and judge them accordingly. Unfortunately this is not always an easy task, for these are precisely the things that 'date' badly and it calls for a considerable effort of the imagination to see them in the light which their creators intended.

And this is what all opera demands of us—imaginative co-operation. Throughout its long history it has been praised and condemned with extravagant enthusiasm. To Dr. Johnson it was merely 'exotic and irrational'; to other men it has appeared frivolous and even morally evil. Yet, at the same time, it has been called 'the noblest spectacle ever devised by man', and composers of all ages have been eager to try their hand at its composition. It has flourished for three hundred and fifty years and shows every sign of continuing to attract the greatest creative minds. For at its heart, when all the frivolities and artificialities have been stripped away, great opera deals with the lasting truths of human character and emotion, and thus must always command our respect and attention.

II

Audiences

JUST as the conventions of opera have changed over the years, so has the behaviour of operatic audiences. The audience of today goes to the opera in a totally different frame of mind from audiences fifty or a hundred or two hundred years ago, expecting different pleasures and according them a very different sort of welcome.

Before public opera houses became the pride and joy of every European city, operas were performed in the palaces of Princes and rich Courtiers, and mostly in celebration of some important event: a wedding or a coronation, for example. Often, members of the Court would themselves take part in the opera—usually in the ballets that formed an important part of the proceedings. Naturally enough, it was expected that on these occasions the opera, besides providing entertainment, would also underline the significance of the event. Thus, an opera performed as part of wedding celebrations would make a point of praising married bliss and faithful love, and go into raptures over the virtues (real or imaginary) of the happy pair. And, of course, the audience would react with appropriate enthusiasm. This sort of opera, intended to flatter an aristocratic patron, lasted well into the eighteenth century—Mozart's *La Clemenza di Tito* was one of the last of the kind, being written in 1791 to celebrate the coronation of Leopold II as King of Bohemia and designed by the government authorities, who chose the libretto, to show the monarchy in a favourable light; presumably in the faint hope of counteracting the sort of doubts aroused by the French Revolution!

The earliest Court Operas were performed in whatever convenient large hall happened to be available. The best seats would be occupied by the Prince and his immediate circle, the next best by the ladies and important foreign visitors, while the rest of the court squeezed in as they could. In some instances a proper theatre was built. For example, the Barberinis, a powerful Roman family, put up a private theatre in 1632, which, we are told, could seat three thousand people. Eventually every Prince came to believe that an opera house was a prime necessity if he was to hold his own in the eyes of other Princes. Some, indeed, went to extremes—Prince Charles Eugene of Württemburg, for example, brought his tiny principality to the verge of bankruptcy trying to outdo his rivals in operatic extravagance.

It is only fair to add that whenever a Prince who had commanded this sort of lavish entertainment was feeling particularly generous, or the entertainment itself had been more than usually successful, he was likely to order several more performances and for one of them would throw open his theatre to the general public. The townspeople might then enter for nothing, to catch a glimpse of how the money produced by their own hard work had been spent!

Within a few years of its birth, however, the idea of opera had caught on to such an extent that it was possible to open a public opera house. This building, the first of its kind, was opened in Venice in 1637 through the private enterprise of two musicians. From this point public opera houses grew up alongside the private court theatres.

In the public opera houses it soon became the practice for wealthy families to hire a group of seats by the season. This had an important influence on the shape that continental opera houses eventually took. Since a wealthy family could reserve part of the theatre for its own exclusive use over a long period it was obviously necessary to be able to mark off that section from the rest of the theatre. Gradually little barriers were introduced to divide off the groups of reserved seats. Soon the barriers rose to make regular walls, and the seats were thus enclosed in a small room, or *box*. In the end the continental opera house came to consist of several layers of boxes piled one on top of the other around the walls of an auditorium shaped like a horse-shoe. Above the top layer of boxes there was an open gallery, while below, in the centre of the horse-shoe, there was an open floor space, or *pit*. Although customs varied from place to place the aristocracy usually sat in the second and third rows of boxes, while the more respectable merchants and their families occupied the layers immediately above. The row of boxes on the same level as the pit floor was often given over to 'ladies of easy virtue'—admitted by the enterprising management as part of the entertainment. The pit itself and the top gallery were open to anyone.

Opera houses soon came to be regarded not only as places of entertainment but as meeting places for the entire city, and, as a result, the audience's standards of behaviour underwent a rapid decline. Boxes were fitted out like small drawing rooms, with chairs and tables. Meals could be taken in them and drink was in constant supply. Some boxes even had private rooms leading off them, into which their owners might retire to play cards or behave in any way they thought fit. In fact boxes were used by their owners as if they were rooms in a private house. The box-owner would arrive, perhaps in the middle of the opera, glance round the theatre to see who was there, acknowledge his friends and then settle down to the main business of the evening—not listening to the music, but chatting with friends, playing cards and dominoes, and so on. In many cities it was customary to go to the opera wearing masks, and this inevitably made the opera house a popular place for intrigue and a happy hunting-ground for unscrupulous adventurers. Government and police spies found them useful centres of information and did not scruple to lurk about, their eyes and ears ready to snap up the slightest detail.

In the public rooms of the theatre there were gaming tables, often run by the less wealthy members of the aristocracy as a profitable source of income. Other rooms were set apart for refreshment. And through all the hubbub the singers performed on the stage, happy in the knowledge that now and again the social life of the theatre would be suspended in favour of a particularly admired aria. For a moment there would be silence, then rapturous applause, and then—society would turn its back until the next highlight.

The behaviour of the singers themselves, however, was scarcely more respectful. When they were not singing they would loll about the stage taking snuff and chatting to their admirers in the nearest boxes, making audible comments on the abilities of the other singers. It was quite possible for a Prima donna's mother to take up a prominent position at the side of the stage, surrounded by her daughter's friends and protectors, holding in her lap such sweetmeats, gargles, mirrors and combs as the songstress might suddenly have need of. But she, of course, when her own turn came, would glide to the centre of the stage, strike an imposing attitude and deliver her aria, sometimes even to the accompaniment of free fights between her own friends in the audience and the supporters of rival singers.

As for the audience in the pit: having paid little to enter they came and went as they pleased, popping in, perhaps, for a single aria. For the most part they were disreputable characters—servants, young thugs looking for adventure, girls offering refreshment and other, more doubtful, wares. In Rome, however, it is reported that any spectator in the pit who made himself too great a nuisance was likely to be seized by the police, taken out and flogged and then brought back to enjoy the rest of the opera!

Nor was this the only danger. The ladies and gentlemen in the upper boxes saw nothing wrong in flinging the un-wanted scraps of their meals into the pit below. If a high Church dignitary happened to be in attendance the more superstitious members of the pit audience would scramble for such refuse as he chose to abandon, cherishing it as 'sacred relics', holding it a sign of grace even to be spat upon. On one occasion the King of Naples amused himself by dropping lumps of greasy macaroni on to the heads of his loyal subjects, who apparently felt it an honour to be thus marked by royal patronage.

In the dimly lit passages that ran behind the boxes matters were, if anything, even less savoury. Here the ser-vants of the box-owners would gather to play dice and drink—and worse, for in a theatre built to hold several thousand people there might, with luck, be two or three lavatories.

The candles which illuminated the theatre, both before and behind the curtain, were made from mutton fat which,

The Ingredients of Opera

besides giving off a peculiarly offensive smell, spread a smoky haze throughout the building which made singers and audience alike cough and spit incessantly. For this reason ladies and gentlemen carried heavily scented 'pomanders' at which they snuffled throughout the performance, the gentlemen only breaking off for a pinch of snuff and the inevitable violent sneeze.

Conditions in the private Court Theatre were, of course, more civilized; but even here it was customary to leave at least one ear open for general conversation, and one eye open to catch the page-boys who circulated with refreshments of all kinds. But with fewer people at least the air was purer.

The behaviour of audiences seems to have reached a peak of extravagance in the early part of the eighteenth century. This is not altogether surprising, for the enormous demand for opera led to a sharp decline in standards. Hack composers were engaged to run up a new work from scraps of older operas—the result was called a 'pasticcio', a musical 'pie'. Favourite librettos were set over and over again, so that audiences scarcely needed to pay attention to the story, for they already knew it by heart. There was little in these operas to encourage attention and good manners.

Probably the rise of comic opera, with its more realistic plot, helped to change the audience's attitude. And certainly the 'reforms' of Gluck and the genius of Mozart produced a style of opera that called for a much greater degree of attention from the audience. Dr. Charles Burney, writing in 1772, commented on the reactions to Gluck's *Alceste*: 'Those who have seen it represented [say it] was so truly theatrical and interesting that they could not keep their eyes off the stage during the whole performance, having their attention so irritated, and their consternation so raised, that they were kept in perpetual anxiety, between hope and fear for the event, till the last scene of the drama.'

Yet it was still possible for him to write of opera in Naples, in the year 1770, that: 'as a spectacle [it] surpasses all that poetry and romance have painted; yet with all this, it must be owned that the magnitude of the building, and the noise of the audience are such that neither the voices nor instruments can be heard distinctly. I was told, however, that on account of the King and Queen being present, the people were much less noisy than on common nights'.

Gradually, however, things began to improve. The rise of romantic grand opera during the early part of the nineteenth century did much to help matters. The stories of these works were more exciting and realistic and the music emphasized these qualities. The general tendency to weld aria and recitative together made it difficult for the audience to turn away from the stage without feeling they had missed something. Further help came from science—in the form of gas lighting, which was introduced in theatres around about 1820. It thus became possible to dim the auditorium lights during the performance, though it did not become customary to extinguish them completely until the very end of the century. Better, cleaner methods of lighting added much to the comfort of singers and audience and made possible a much greater range of lighting effects on the stage itself. And all these considerations had the effect of concentrating the audience's attention where it belonged—on the stage.

Yet it must not be supposed that this change of attitude took place overnight. It was still common for the audience to arrive late, chatter its way through the overture, use its

The Ingredients of Opera

boxes as social centres, divide itself into rival and noisy factions over the favourite singers. As late as 1875 Verdi was able to cause annoyance and dismay simply by placing a particularly beautiful aria too early in his opera *Aida* for the habitual late-comers. While Wagner, in 1861, caused a riot among the members of the fashionable 'Jockey Club' who arrived half-way through the first Paris performance of *Tannhäuser* to find that the Ballet had already been performed—Wagner, for dramatic reasons, had placed it at the beginning of the work instead of in the second or third acts.

Indeed, it is to Wagner that much of our present-day respect for opera is due. He demanded that his works should receive the same attention as a Beethoven symphony; that the doors should be closed to late-comers; that the house lights should be dimmed; that the audience should not applaud when and where it liked; that scenic effects should work as smoothly as possible; that everyone and everything connected with the opera should be devoted to one end—the performance of a masterpiece. It might also be added that the sheer weight of his orchestration and the size and grandeur of his works generally, tended to stun his audiences into submission. Wagner's own opera house, at Bayreuth, was built in such a way as to underline the sort of attitude he expected from his audience. Eventually, even in Italy, a modified version of his ideals came to be accepted as part and parcel of ordinary theatrical good manners.

Though audiences are still inclined to 'dress up' for opera they do so nowadays more out of respect for the occasion than through any desire to show off their social position. Two world wars have knocked a great deal of the false glamour out of 'society' and its hangers-on. Opera houses no longer blaze with diamond-studded ladies, and

18

gentlemen resplendent in their orders and decorations. Perhaps on gala occasions something of this returns; but the day-to-day audience goes to the opera because it loves the music and not because it wishes to be seen. Within living memory audiences at the Metropolitan Opera House of New York felt quite justified in complaining against operas like *Il Trovatore* that made too great a use of the darkened stage, on the grounds that their jewels could no longer sparkle to such devastating effect. Today the question simply does not arise.

A similar change can be seen in the attitude of audiences to the singers. The great artists of eighteenth-century opera received the same sort of rapturous following that some present-day teenagers lavish on their favourite pop-singers. No reward was too extravagant and many of them were able to accumulate handsome fortunes for the comfort of their declining years. The great singers of the nineteenth century, and indeed singers up till the First World War, enjoyed a vast and enthusiastic following. The Melbas and the Carusos, the Destinns and the de Reszkes demanded, and received, fabulous salaries from the glittering society that hung upon their golden notes. They represented the stage at its most glamorous and their supporters were only too happy to pay tribute.

Today, the opera star has lost much ground to the stars of pop music and the film world. They have, of course, their personal following and still command appropriately large rewards for their artistry, but the furore that attends their success is no longer so overwhelming. Present-day audiences are more democratic in their praise, bestowing it as readily upon the composer, the conductor, the stage designer and the producer as upon the great singer. And the change is all to the good.

III

The Opera Singer

UNTIL the invention of the film star the opera singer
enjoyed an almost undisputed position in the mind
of the general public as a figure of enormous and enviable
glamour. The glitter and romance of their careers outshone
even the triumphs of the great actors and actresses of the
ordinary theatre. Indeed, everything was in their favour.
Opera was an art well up in the social scale and its patrons
were eager to lavish rewards upon their favourites. The
splendour of the opera houses themselves, the grandeur of
operatic performances and, above all, the irresistible thrill
of great music all contributed to the enchantment. And, to
give them their due, the great opera stars of the past played
up to the occasion. The gentlemen displayed remarkable
temperament and struck imposing attitudes; the ladies
covered themselves in jewels and fine clothes and allowed
themselves a troupe of breathless admirers. They were
fine figures and they knew it.

At different periods, of course, public idolatry of opera
singers has taken different forms. In the eighteenth century it was directed towards that extraordinary phen-
omenon the *Castrato*, or artificial male soprano. For the
most part these singers were children of humble parents
and had been sold (because of their parents' poverty) to

some music teacher, or musical academy, in the faint hope that, after the appropriate operation, their voices might develop sufficiently for them to join the ranks of great singers. Sometimes the parents scraped together enough money to pay for the wretched child's musical education themselves, and then presumably looked upon the whole sorry affair as an investment that might one day pay off handsome dividends. Unfortunately not every promising voice developed sufficiently, and then the plight of the mutilated child scarcely bears thinking about. But for the 'lucky' few the rewards were immense. The greatest among them, men like Caffarelli and Farinelli, were able to retire enormously wealthy, honoured throughout Europe.

Perhaps, of all the castrati, Farinelli achieved the greatest success and has left the most enduring legend. In London alone he earned sums of money (something in the region of £5,000 a year) that in eighteenth-century terms were quite without precedent. 'One God, one Farinelli,' cried one lady of fashion, overcome by his artistry, and the rest of Society echoed her. In 1737 he was invited by the Queen of Spain to come to Madrid in the hope that his exquisite singing would soothe the mind of King Philip V, who was suffering from such acute depression that he could scarcely be persuaded to take the slightest interest in even the most urgent affairs of his country. The plan succeeded and Farinelli remained in Madrid, singing, so it is said, the same four songs to the King each night for nine years! He remained in Madrid even after King Philip had died, and acquired an immense influence at court—which, it is pleasant to note, he never abused. He retired to Italy in 1759, living out his old age in great splendour.

Castrati eventually disappeared from the opera houses, at least as a regular feature, about 1825 when the Tenor—

The Ingredients of Opera

Baritone–Bass pattern of male voices came to be accepted as the proper complement to Sopranos and Contraltos.

The honours now went to the ladies—sopranos such as Malibran, Grisi, Jenny Lind and Patti. Something of the enthusiasm they aroused can be seen from this description of Madame Patti's departure from Covent Garden after celebrating her twenty-fifth annual appearance there:

> After the performance an extraordinary scene took place outside the theatre. A band and a number of torch bearers had assembled at the northern entrance in Hart Street, awaiting Madame Patti's departure. When she stepped into her carriage it was headed by the bearers of the lighted torches; and as the carriage left the band struck up. An enormous crowd very soon gathered; and it gradually increased in numbers as the procession moved on. . . . The noise, and the glare of the coloured lights, and the cracking of fireworks which were let off every now and then, aroused men, women, and children from their beds . . .

Madame Patti must have been delighted by this demonstration, especially as she had just been presented with a superb diamond bracelet.

Nowadays such demonstrations are aroused only by a very different class of singer. But it is really not so long ago that the Melbas and the Carusos were inspiring similar raptures, and, even today, the arrival of a Maria Callas or a Joan Sutherland can capture the headlines. In a world where the ordinary theatre looks for its material in kitchen-sink drama and the squalor of feckless domesticity, opera still retains its grand manner and air of unreality. Even the most realistic of modern operas cannot escape this magic—the music sees to that. And opera singers, though no longer the idols they once were, still have their glamour.

It would, however, be very wrong to suppose that the

actual business of being an opera singer was all romance and delight. Opera singers may look like creatures of fairy tale when they are on the stage, but the facts behind their daily work speak of a very different sort of reality.

There are three essentials to a successful operatic career: talent, good health and self-discipline. Most singers in England begin by studying privately with a singing teacher, who may well be a soloist of considerable standing. The business of deciding to specialize in opera is largely a matter of temperament: some people feel drawn to the operatic stage and nothing will satisfy them until they reach it. The next step is to enter one of the London musical training centres, perhaps the Royal Academy, or the Royal College of Music. Here the young singer will receive a training of anything up to four years that covers voice production, musical appreciation, theory, training in some instrument (usually the piano) and certain specific training in operatic stage work. The recently formed National School of Opera concentrates, as its name suggests, entirely upon operatic problems and includes in its training programme such matters as make-up and deportment and other skills that come within the scope of a 'drama school'.

At the same time the young singer will seek out every opportunity to hear great artists, either in the flesh or on gramophone records, and will study all the important operatic rôles. Both Sadler's Wells and Covent Garden contribute their share to the student's education by reserving for them certain places in their theatres where, free of charge, they can hear the opera and follow a score at the same time.

Gradually the young singer will come to understand the many different kinds of interpretation that can be put upon what might once have seemed a straightforward rôle, and, with a little experience and help from a teacher, will learn to distinguish between the good and the bad.

The first steps of an English operatic singer's career, once student days are left behind, are particularly difficult. They sound simple enough: 'join an opera company'. But in England, with two permanent opera houses in London, a summer opera at Glyndebourne, and precious little else, the competition is almost overwhelming. Though foreign opera companies might have an opening for a specially gifted English singer, they naturally give priority to their own people. There is little point in hoping for early experience abroad.

However, the position is not entirely hopeless. Vacancies do occur and, with the increasing interest in radio and television opera, the numerous Festivals of Music that have popped up all over the country and, if all else fails, the possibility of joining the chorus of some 'musical', the young singer may, with luck, land on his feet—at the bottom of the ladder.

Starting as a member of the chorus the young singer may move on to small parts and so graduate to solo rôles and a name that the audience remembers. But it is hard work. There are few lucky breaks to launch an unknown voice from the back row of the chorus to overnight stardom. For the most part an opera singer's life is a tale of unremitting study, constant practice and endless hard work. And until the distant final heights are reached the rewards are not spectacular. Most singers find it necessary to give concert recitals, sing in paid choirs and work for radio and recording companies—when the circumstances of the job permit. The top international stars may command anything from £250 to £1,000 a performance, but the average soloist will be lucky to earn £25 a week.

The Opera Singer

Opera house routine usually involves the singers in a performance and a three-hour morning rehearsal each day for six days a week. The afternoons are left free, and any singer with a taxing rôle to sing during the evening will most probably snatch at them for relaxation. For singing is a most tiring occupation—not only because of the demands it makes on the spirit, so that the singer may bring to each performance the same freshness and vitality, but in sheer physical effort. The only weapons the singer has are an assured technique and thorough self-discipline.

It can also be imagined that the pursuit of good health is one of the major preoccupations in a singer's life. Coughs and colds and physical exhaustion must be avoided at all costs. This may not be an easy matter when there are draughty dressing rooms to be fought against, long journeys to be made when on tour, and all the thousand and one difficulties to be faced when living in a large capital city.

Then there are all the problems connected with the performance itself. An opera singer must act as well as sing. He must learn to do both, even though he is clad in an awkward costume and weighed down by a cumbersome helmet or stifled in an unaccustomed beard. He must learn to keep one eye on the conductor without letting the audience know that this is what he is doing. He must have at least a working knowledge of the other rôles in each opera so that he may make his contribution as part of a team.

As we shall see, the preparation of a new work generally takes about four weeks. The singer will probably need two weeks to learn a new part, going through it over and over again with the 'repetiteur' until it is safely lodged in the memory. Then come the general rehearsals, the costume fittings and at last the dress rehearsal. A day's rest follows, and then—the first night.

Once an opera is in the repertory it is not rehearsed again unless it has not been performed for at least six months. The singer, of course, will run through his part at home just to be on the safe side. And most singers like to keep up regular lessons, for it is all too easy to develop bad singing habits. The teacher can keep an eye on such lapses and so save the singer endless embarrassment, and even check the gradual ruination of a good voice.

With all these chilling observations it may well seem as if the opera singer's lot is an exceptionally unhappy one. But for the singer who learns to rise above the problems and master the difficulties it is not so—the thrill of singing in opera is compensation enough.

IV

The Composer

FEW composers seem to have been able to resist the temptation to try their hand at opera. There is something about it, the challenge, perhaps, of finding music to express definite ideas, that has appealed to all sorts and conditions of composers ever since the idea was first put forward at the beginning of the seventeenth century. Yet it is hardly a challenge to be taken up lightly. The history of opera is strewn thick with failures: out of the thousands upon thousands of works that have been composed only a very few have survived as undisputed masterpieces.

Curiously, however, it has not always been the greatest masters, in the purely intellectual sense, that have proved to be the most successful opera composers. For in this art one special gift is needed that does not always go hand in hand with creative musical talent. That gift is the power to create drama in terms of music. If the composer has no feeling for the theatre, no instinct for dramatic pace and no ability to express these things in terms of music, then, though he may write great symphonies and concertos, he will fail when it comes to opera.

The great composer of opera must also be a great dramatist. He must be able to create characters through his music, paint pictures and describe events. His music must not only serve the words he sets, but add to their meaning and so reveal the inner nature of his characters and the drama in which they are involved. This cannot be done merely by sprinkling a number of pretty tunes throughout the work and then hoping for the best—though some operas have been little more than this. The great opera has a musical shape as well as a dramatic shape, even though the music cannot stand without the drama.

And here, perhaps, the greatest dangers lie. At best the marriage between words and music is uneasy. Music is a language in its own right and, as such, obeys its own nature; it therefore does not always take kindly to the methods of verbal thought. If the composer wishes to respect the words of his libretto down to the last detail he must make a corresponding sacrifice in his musical language—something of this can be seen in Debussy's *Pelléas and Mélisande*, or Vaughan Williams' *Riders to the Sea*, both of which were based on plays that were poetic masterpieces in their own right. If, on the other hand, he decides in favour of the music, then the effect of the words *as words* must, to some extent, be sacrificed. We find this choice most evident in Wagner's Music Dramas. Most composers, however, attempt some sort of compromise, so that at different moments words and music take precedence one over the other.

The business of writing an opera is complex and long drawn out. In the first place the composer must choose a story which can be given a suitable dramatic shape. During the seventeenth and eighteenth centuries the choice was often made for him. He would be commissioned, say, to write an opera for a special occasion. Obviously, even if he wasn't told by his patrons what subject would be acceptable for their entertainment he had to find something that would not cause offence. For example, most of Lully's operas were written for performance before King Louis XIV of France. Each one, therefore, opened with a stately prologue in which the King's supposed virtues were praised beyond mere flattery. The remainder of the work was devoted to a number of characters who, in the intervals of various improbable adventures, would make the sort of remarks that might also be taken as compliments to the royal patron. If Lully could please the King then no one else would dare to criticize.

By the nineteenth century commissions were given with a fairly free hand. When the Khedive of Egypt asked Verdi for an opera to celebrate the opening of the Suez Canal he went so far as to ask that the subject might be Egyptian, but he left the final choice of *Aida* to the composer. Nowadays even official commissions are given with a free hand, though common sense will tell the composer that his subject must be appropriate to the occasion. One interesting example may make this point clear: when Benjamin Britten was asked to write an opera to be performed before Queen Elizabeth II during the coronation celebrations he chose a story of Queen Elizabeth I and the Earl of Essex. Obviously the subject was appropriate, but it was certainly not designed to flatter monarchy, and stuffier members of the establishment were rather put out by the choice.

From Gluck and Mozart onwards it became increasingly the practice for composers to make operas only from the stories that genuinely moved them. Previously, if the work had not been commissioned, the stories tended to be in keeping with current fashion and this was laid down, more often than not, by poets and dramatists rather than composers. Once composers began to insist on stories that genuinely aroused their emotions they began to emerge as great dramatists themselves.

During the past two hundred years, then, the choice of subject has been left mainly to the composer. Any number of things may influence him: he may be swept away by enthusiasm for a current dramatic or literary fashion, as Weber was when he produced the horror-story romanticism of *Der Freischütz*; or he may, like Beethoven with *Fidelio*, wish to portray a particularly admirable type of character. He may, as Puccini did with *Madame Butterfly*, fall in love with a stage play—or a poem, as Britten did with *Peter Grimes*. Novels, legends, Bible stories, incidents from real life, almost anything, in fact, can spark off the composer's imagination so that he feels he must bring the drama to life through his music.

Sometimes the initial suggestion for an opera comes from outside: both of Verdi's last masterpieces, *Otello* and *Falstaff*, were suggested by his friend and librettist the composer Arrigo Boito. Obviously, in this case, Boito had a very shrewd idea of what would interest Verdi and bring out the best in him. Puccini pressed all his friends into service and had them reading plays and novels by the dozen in the hope of finding the perfect subject (in the end, though, he rejected most of their suggestions in favour of his own discoveries). Sometimes the composer's publisher will suggest there is a market for a certain type of opera. An opera house may ask for a work especially to suit its own company and stage resources. A great singer may demand, or inspire, the creation of a new rôle, tailored to her personality and abilities. But in the end, whatever the external promptings may be, it is certain that no composer will ever begin so arduous a task unless he is himself completely convinced by his theme.

The Composer

Once a story has been decided upon the first stage in the actual work is the preparation of a *scenario*—that is to say, a detailed outline of the story and the manner in which it can best be put over on the stage. Sometimes the composer will make this sketch himself (Britten, for example, drafted the first outline of *Peter Grimes*). The scenario is then taken over by the librettist, whose job it is to make an operatic play for the composer to set to music.

His task is not an easy one. He has to find words that will tell the story adequately and yet leave room for the music to blossom in its own special way. He must satisfy his own literary instincts and yet provide words that will stimulate the composer. Altogether the odds against anyone ever satisfying these conflicting requirements have caused many a composer to wish he could write his own libretti, as Wagner and Berlioz did. A glance at any opera composer's life-history will reveal as one of his major burdens the search for the ideal librettist.

In earlier days, when opera was written according to a settled convention of arias in alternation with recitatives, the librettist's problems were few. It was generally agreed that the main characters should have a certain number of arias in each act and that each aria should present a different kind of emotion. The arias themselves followed a basic pattern and required only a few simple words that might be repeated according to the needs of the composer's tune. For example, the words of the aria: 'Love in her eyes sits playing', from Handel's *Acis and Galatea*, consist of the following eight lines:

> Love in her eyes sits playing
> And sheds delicious death;
> Love in her lips is straying,
> And warbling in her breath.

The Ingredients of Opera

Love on her breast sits panting,
And swells with soft desire.
No grace, no charm is wanting,
To set the heart on fire.

The words express only one emotion: that of the hero's love for the heroine; they do little more and certainly cannot be said to portray character. By repeating the words Handel manages to spread these simple lines over an aria of seventy bars. To set the same eight lines in the same rhythm, but without repeating any words, would take up a mere eight bars! It is not entirely unfair to say that in the eighteenth century the librettist's problems came to little more than the need to turn out a supply of elegant verse which might be strung together in reasonable dramatic outline.

From Gluck and Mozart onwards the demands made upon the librettist have increased steadily, so that nowadays he is looked upon as a near equal with the composer in the creation of a satisfying opera. Audiences now expect that operatic stories should be more than just a peg to hang attractive arias on, and as realistic and truthful to human experience as possible. The words must therefore suggest and help the music to suggest character in all its human complexity. It is no longer enough for the hero to say that he is in love—he has to behave like a human being in love, with all the contradictions this involves. At the same time the librettist is denied some of the resources of the ordinary dramatist since he has to leave room for the music to function as music. His libretto is therefore something in the nature of a detailed sketch which the music can expand and bring to perfection. This is why even a modern libretto makes poor reading on its own account. It has been constructed as a partner to the music and in such a way that it can come to life only when clothed in that music.

This basic requirement has been true of libretti ever since opera began. For example: when, in *Dido and Aeneas*, Dido takes her farewell of life, Purcell creates a magnificent and deeply moving aria from the simple words:

> When I am laid in earth, may my wrongs create
> No trouble in thy breast. Remember me, but ah!
> Forget my fate.

Read aloud, the words are hopelessly inadequate to the tragic situation. But they are precisely suitable as a skeleton for Purcell's music, and clothed in this become a noble and utterly convincing expression of grief. Had the words been too fine in themselves there might have been nothing left for the music to add. For example, when Shakespeare's Cleopatra takes her farewell of life she does so in a passage of great poetic beauty, beginning:

> Give me my robes, put on my crown; I have
> Immortal longings in me . . .

To such words the addition of music would not only be inappropriate, but impertinent and totally ineffective.

The librettist, then, must be a man of creative ability who is willing to play a modest rôle. He must not overwhelm his composer with self-sufficient poetry; he must spin words that cry out for music.

Having once found this rare chap most composers have still kept a watchful eye on his work. In fact it is true to say that composers themselves play an important part in shaping the details of a libretto. Here, for example, is Mozart, writing to his father in 1781 about the opera *Die Entführung aus dem Serail*:

The Ingredients of Opera

. . . As the original text began with a monologue, I asked Herr Stephanie to make a little arietta out of it—and then to put in a duet instead of making the two chatter together after Osmin's short song. As we have given the part of Osmin to Herr Fischer, who certainly has an excellent bass voice (in spite of the fact that the Archbishop told me that he sang too low for a bass and that I assured him that he would sing higher next time), we must take advantage of it, particularly as he has the whole of the Viennese public on his side. But in the original libretto Osmin has only this short song and nothing else to sing, except in the trio and the finale; so he has been given another aria in Act I and is to have another in Act II. I have explained to Stephanie the words I require for this aria—indeed I had finished composing the music for it before Stephanie knew anything about it . . .

The dramatist in Mozart has raced ahead of his librettist, forcing him to write music for an aria that his instincts tell him he must have. Mozart follows up these remarks with a description of the shape of Osmin's aria and, in the process, shows how the music can suggest details of an emotion that the words need only touch upon:

. . . as Osmin's rage gradually increases, there comes (just when the aria seems to be at an end) the *allegro assai*, which is in a totally different measure and in a different key; this is bound to be very effective. For just as a man in such a towering rage oversteps all the bounds of order, moderation and propriety, and completely forgets himself, so must the music forget itself too . . .

Nearly a hundred years later we find Verdi writing to the librettist of *Aida* in much the same detail:

I have an idea for the consecration scene . . . which should consist of a Litany chanted by the priestesses, to which the priests respond. Then a sacred dance to slow and sad music, followed by a short recitative, energetic and solemn like a biblical psalm. Finally a prayer of two strophes for the Chief Priest and repeated by everyone. You will see that it would have a quiet and pathetic character, distinguishing it from the other choruses at the end of the first scene and in the second finale, which smack a little of the 'Marseillaise'.

A little later Verdi sent his librettist a rough sketch for the words of an aria, with the request that he make something similar only better, and adding:

You have no idea what a lovely melody can be made out of this . . .

Evidently he too had written the music in advance.

Most libretti are literally hammered into shape. Eric Crozier, who collaborated with the novelist E. M. Forster in writing the libretto for Benjamin Britten's opera *Billy Budd*, has left it on record that their work went through five different stages. First, they talked over the subject with the composer and drew up a list of characters and a rough outline of the dramatic shape. A few weeks later they prepared a short version of the plot and divided the action into its various scenes. Then came a third manuscript, which can be thought of as the first draft of the words that were eventually used. Britten brooded over this for six months and then, with the two librettists, proceeded to hammer out the libretto from which he was to compose. Presumably his mind had already begun to shape some of the musical ideas and this in turn helped him to mould the libretto into the form he needed. The fifth and last version came from the composer and represents all the tiny alteration of details that the actual process of composition had forced him to make in the working draft.

The Ingredients of Opera

The actual composition of an opera, which may take anything up to two or three years, does not always proceed in an orderly fashion with the composer religiously setting the libretto word for word, starting at the beginning and ploughing through to the end. From the moment he has decided to write a particular opera the composer's brain is likely to weave ideas which will influence the dramatic shape of the work and even its melodic details. It is probably true to say that the real inspiration for an opera is the composer's and that he must extract from the patient librettist the sort of libretto he needs to make this inspiration come true.

There is no reason why a composer should begin his musical work by tackling the first scene of his opera first. Tchaikovsky, for example, began work on *Eugen Onegin* by composing the famous 'Letter Scene', which he felt to be the emotional heart of the work. An opera, in fact, is like a large tapestry. The composer knows what the whole picture will be like when he has finished and can therefore start wherever he likes, dodging about from point to point as his inspiration compels him. But it is essential that his mind should grasp the structure of the opera as a whole, so that ultimately he can weld the various bits and pieces into a single musical unity.

The actual business of writing down the music is usually done in the form of a piano 'sketch'. Some of Wagner's first drafts are drawn on a single staff, with reminders added here and there about the orchestration. Certain harmonic passages he worked out in detail. At this stage in the composition Wagner was accustomed to use the piano in order to test his ideas and often placed his manuscript paper on the piano lid, writing with his right hand while his left hand tried out the ideas as they formed in his mind.

In more complex passages, however, he would write the music direct into full orchestral score.

Other men, Mozart and Britten are examples, assemble their music in their heads and write it down only when they have thought it to a state of perfection!

In the end, of course, it hardly matters how the composer sets about his task. Whatever method he chooses he cannot escape an enormous amount of hard work. Simply to write out the orchestral score, which may contain anything from five hundred to a thousand or more pages, is in itself a fearful undertaking. And as for the labour of actual creation—this is scarcely to be calculated.

When at last the score is complete it is handed over to the copyists, who make out the individual orchestral parts and arrange a piano reduction for publication and generally see to it that everything is to hand for the singers and musicians to translate the composer's blue-print into living sound and drama.

V

The Opera House

IF there is one point upon which both critics and admirers of opera will be found to agree it is that opera spells money. Indeed, its entire history is littered with tales of financial disaster; of Princes who have annoyed their subjects by pouring State revenue into private opera houses; of composers who have turned to theatrical management and inevitable bankruptcy; of wily, hard-headed impresarios brought to despair by a sudden change in operatic taste. Yet, to be fair, it must also be admitted that opera can create fortunes as well as lose them. Theatres have been built on the strength of great operatic successes; favourite singers have retired in luxury, weighed down with jewels and furs; and even a few composers have contrived to amass vast fortunes through writing successful operas (Puccini, for example, died practically a millionaire).

Nowadays, though composers and singers may still earn enviable sums, the actual production of opera must always be carried on at a loss. The sudden discovery of this fact is enough to throw the opponents of opera in a great rage and cause them to write strong letters to the daily newspapers, for they know that if an art form can only be carried on at a loss it must be subsidized and, in the absence of opera-crazy millionaires, the subsidy must come from public funds.

The Opera House

Now all civilized nations have accepted that national prestige owes as much to the Art a country produces as to its material successes. A nation that can boast of no artistic ability can hardly claim to play a part in civilization. Curiously, it is to the Arts of byegone civilizations that we look when we try to estimate their contribution to the progress of mankind, for it is in Art that we see the soul of a people reflected and intensified. And so most nations choose to support the efforts of their artists (modestly, of course), recognizing that they are the true mirror of the national soul.

The granting of subsidies to opera perhaps causes greater annoyance to some people because they feel it to be an aristocratic art form. Few people complain about the cost of Public Libraries, Art Galleries and Museums. Opera, however, has an air of exclusiveness—due, one can only suppose, to its long history of aristocratic patronage. In point of fact it is no more exclusive than a football match.

To the average Englishman this is not an easy point of view to accept. In Italy and Germany, where each town of any size actively supports its own opera house, the question does not arise. There, opera is a fact of daily life. But in this country, with only three public opera houses (if you count Glyndebourne), it is hardly surprising that opera should be thought to appeal only to a small minority and that complaints should arise whenever there is any question of supporting it with public money. Yet the fact remains that operas can only be produced at a loss, for the whole mechanics of their production goes against the possibility of any profit.

More than any other theatrical set-up the opera house is a world on its own. It calls on a wider variety of servants, and operates under more peculiarly limited conditions than any other theatre and, in consequence, cannot properly be judged by ordinary theatrical standards. Take, as an example, the facts behind the Royal Opera House, Covent Garden—London's leading opera house and one of the finest in the world today.

The present building dates from 1858 and stands on a site previously occupied by two earlier opera houses, which were burned to the ground in 1808 and 1856 respectively. The first of these theatres had been built in 1732 by John Rich out of the profits, it is said, of *The Beggar's Opera*, which he brought to the stage in 1728.

In most European capitals the opera house usually occupies a commanding position in some magnificent square. Not so Covent Garden. In itself a fine building, it lies trapped in a huddle of narrow streets between a crowded vegetable market and Bow Street Police Station. But this was not the intention of the architects. The square in which the vegetable market stands was once a magnificent open space, surrounded by fine arcaded houses in the Italian style. At the centre of the design stood Inigo Jones's St. Paul's Church. It was intended that opera-goers should walk about in the arcaded square during the intervals, imagining themselves, perhaps, in the Italy of the opera they patronized. This ambitious and beautiful scheme came to little, however, and was soon swallowed up in the demands of commerce—an event which is curiously symbolic of the whole history of opera in this country. Yet there *is* something to be said in favour of Covent Garden's ungainly surroundings, for the bustle of the market men does at least anchor the grandeurs of opera firmly in the facts of everyday life.

Unlike the ordinary theatre an opera house does not prepare a single work in the expectation that it will enjoy a long run. It is, rather, a showcase for a large repertory of classical masterpieces which must be changed constantly. The ordinary theatrical manager invests in a single play and, if he has been wise in his choice, can then sit back during a long run while the profits come pouring in. Save for the day-to-day running costs of his theatre he has no more expenses. After a certain degree of popularity his play is bound to bring him a profit. But the opera house must prepare some half-dozen works for each season, so that no one opera is repeated on consecutive evenings. Over the years new operas are introduced, partly to replace the less successful operas of previous seasons and partly because it is essential to present a view of the entire operatic repertory. No management that played safe by relying upon the same handful of sure-fire successes, year in year out, would remain in office long. Right from the beginning, then, the opera house has to make an initial investment in the year's work that is far in excess of any ordinary theatre. At the same time the returns for each individual opera are only gathered in over a long period.

Again, opera is a more complex art form than ordinary drama. To present it all the resources of the dramatic theatre are needed, plus all the resources of a concert hall. And, on top of this, extra resources are needed to link these two aspects together. The average opera may call for an orchestra of sixty to a hundred players, a chorus of fifty or more singers, and anything up to a dozen principal singers. In the background there must be a vast army of scene-shifters, electricians, painters and carpenters, wardrobe staff and costume makers, administrators, programme sellers, cleaners and heaven knows what more besides.

For example, during the year 1960–61 Covent Garden

had on its payroll a staff of 838 persons. This was split up into the following groups: Orchestra, 124 players; Solo Artists and Management, 229 persons; 202 Stage and Staff Hands; an Administration and Front of House Staff of 134; and 149 'others'. Naturally this roll, which by operatic standards is by no means large, added up to a considerable sum when it came to paying the wages—actually some £892,024.

During the same year the total expenditure came to £1,410,003. Total receipts amounted only to £940,292. A Government Grant, administered by the Arts Council of Great Britain, came to £500,737. Thus the opera house was left with a 'surplus' of £31,026—or, if you prefer to ignore the subsidy as an unfair source of income, a deficit of £469,711.

Nor should it for one moment be thought that Covent Garden's inability to balance its books without the aid of a subsidy was in any way due to inefficiency or a poor standard of performance, or even the unpopularity of the works it presented. Their production of *Peter Grimes* drew 95% houses, while even so difficult a work as *Wozzeck* attracted a 78% audience (only eight years before the same work had played to a mere 38%). As for standards of performance, Covent Garden now ranks as one of the world's leading opera houses. The fact is that even if every seat were sold throughout the year the expense of running the theatre could not be met and a subsidy would still be needed. A possible answer might be to raise the price of seats, but it is extremely doubtful if this would do more than drive away irreplaceable members of the audience.

The cost of setting up individual operas varies. A new work, or a new production of an important but unusual classic, will, of course, be more expensive than the production of a popular standard classic. Covent Garden's 1960 productions will illustrate this point. A routine classic, Rossini's *Barber of Seville*, was mounted at a cost of £7,931. An out-of-the-ordinary classic, Bellini's *La Sonnambula*, cost nearly double at £15,172. A completely new work, Britten's *Midsummer Night's Dream*, came to £15,686— and drew bigger houses than either of the other two.

Covent Garden, however, has special financial difficulties that do not occur in the running of most opera houses. Although it is looked upon as a National Opera House, the State does not in fact own the theatre, but leases it from a private company: Covent Garden Properties Limited. In turn, the State sub-lets the theatre to the Royal Opera House, Covent Garden Limited, which is a non-profit-distributing company organized to run the building as an opera house. The actual cost of rent, rates, insurance and maintenance comes to something in the region of £100,000 each year (this includes the expense of renting other buildings for storing scenery, office work and rehearsal). Apart from being an enormous financial millstone the fact that the theatre is owned by a private landlord means that neither the owner, nor the State, nor the Covent Garden company are very anxious to spend the sort of money on repairs and maintenance that such a vast and elderly building requires. In this way it remains somewhat inefficient as a building, for in some respects it is hopelessly out of date.

It must also be obvious that any opera house working an extensive repertory needs special equipment over and above that carried by the normal theatre. In terms of space alone the problems are considerable. There must be room in the orchestra pit for anything up to a full-scale Wagnerian orchestra—that is to say, a hundred or more players.

The Ingredients of Opera

The stage must be large enough to take spectacular scenery and a large number of performers. It must also be well enough equipped to produce all kinds of unusual effects —trap doors, hydraulic lifts, the cyclorama and all manner of electrical devices come in here. And because performances must change throughout the week it is essential to have space enough to store several sets of scenery and stage props and hang up the hundreds of costumes that will be needed for the season's work. Everything must be ready to hand, stored neatly and safely for immediate use.

To cope with these problems there are stage-hands, carpenters, scene-painters and wardrobe staff. When they are not going through the routine work connected with current productions these admirable technicians are engaged in creating the conditions for the new productions— the painter in the paint shop immediately above the stage, the costume-makers and carpenters in various workrooms in and about the theatre.

At the head of all this effort is the General Administrator. He is responsible for the overall planning of work and policy, business and financial affairs and the appointment of staff. Usually he has as his right-hand man a Musical Director, who is also the Chief Conductor and responsible for all artistic decisions, including the appointment of singers and orchestral players and, most important of all, the choice of operatic repertoire.

In this last capacity the Musical Director has many points to consider. He cannot choose an opera simply because he likes it himself. Since one of the functions of the great opera house is to act as a musuem for the operatic masterpieces of the past, its repertory must provide a balanced picture of operatic history. There must be room for Mozart as well as Puccini, for Wagner as well as Verdi;

the great comic masterpieces of Rossini must appear alongside the tragedies of Gluck. And, most important of all,
there must be room for the works of living composers. The
Musical Director must also consider whether the opera he
has in mind will suit the talents of his company—though,
of course, he may sign on special guest artists if he needs
them. He must also consider whether or not the work will
suit his theatre—a small-scale, intimate work would appear
lost in a theatre as large as Covent Garden. Then he must
find the right singers for the parts and the right Conductor
to guide them to a sympathetic interpretation of the music.
He must choose a Producer and Stage Designer who are
likely to understand its theatrical needs. Above all, however much he may dislike the idea, he must consider
whether the opera he hopes to perform will pay its way
sufficiently to justify the effort and expense that must
inevitably be involved.

To the Musical Director also falls the task of getting
together and training the orchestra. As Chief Conductor
he rehearses the soloists, chorus and orchestra of each work
he is himself directing, and supervises the preparation of
those works he has handed over to other conductors. To
help him in this task there is a staff of Assistant Conductors
who will conduct certain performances themselves and, in
the meantime, act as coaches (repetiteurs) to the singers.
A Chorus Master is also on the music staff and in charge
of the chorus.

Equally important, though easily forgotten, is the Music
Librarian. He looks after all the music in the opera house,
seeing to it that nothing is missing when it comes to the
performance, replacing lost orchestral parts, marking in
cuts and changes of interpretation, and so forth.

On the dramatic side of opera production are the various

theatre technicians, whose presence is just as essential to the success of the work as that of the musicians. In charge of production is the Stage Director, or Producer, as he is sometimes called. He controls the movement of singers on the stage, arranging things in such a way as to underline the dramatic and musical meaning of the work. At his right hand is the Stage Designer, who designs the scenery and the costumes—ensuring that they are both convincing and easy to handle. Another important ally is the Chief Electrician, who must light the stage in a way that is in keeping with the needs of the opera. His job also includes the creation of all the special effects that turn up in the more romantic operas—the storms and tempests, the moonlight and mystery.

During the actual performance, however, the man in charge of everything that happens on the stage is the Stage Manager. Once the opera is ready for the public the Producer retires from the scene, leaving his idea of how the work should be done in the hands of those who must actually bring it to life. The Stage Director works from a large script in which all the Producer's directions are noted down—from the singers' movements, to the lighting cues and operation of stage machinery.

To complete the opera house staff there remain only those men and women who work under the House Manager at the 'front of the house'. These will include the Box Office staff, who arrange publicity as well as the printing and sale of tickets and programmes, the programme sellers, barmen, cloakroom attendants, commissionaires, cleaners and firemen.

All in all it is an impressive and extraordinarily diverse collection of people. Each carries out his appointed task so that the complicated machinery that lies behind every operatic production can glide smoothly into action. That we, the audience, tend to forget their existence is, perhaps, the greatest tribute they can receive: for their aim is not to push forward their individual gifts, but to bring to life a work of art.

VI

Preparing the Opera

S O far we have been concerned with the personalities involved in the day-to-day running of the opera house. Now we must spare a thought for the routine itself.

Like all complex organizations the opera house works to a schedule, planned ahead so that no time is wasted and no one is left wondering what they ought to be doing. The difficulties in staging an opera are so great that it is essential to make plans far in advance of the first night. Indeed, any sensible management will have its plans laid at least a year in advance. After all, imagine the decisions that have to be made!

The General Administrator and the Musical Director, after weighing up the evidence for and against a new production, must then set about the business of finding suitable performers for the various rôles. If for some reason they cannot supply the entire cast from the members of their own resident company, they must look around for a Guest Star—perhaps someone who has previously distinguished himself in foreign productions of the same work. Immediately there begins all the bother of finding out if the guest is free and willing to sing, and if so at what fee and under what conditions. If the potential guest is particularly famous then competition will be enormous and plans must be laid even further ahead than usual. Any management that relied upon being able to get hold of a great singer at, say, three months' notice would soon find itself out of business. The same problems arise when guest Conductors, Producers and Designers are needed. If several guests are to be called in then the problem of co-ordinating the dates on which they can be free becomes a nightmare of telephone calls, letters and telegrams, tentative acceptances and last-minute refusals.

Once these details have been fixed the planning of a new production proceeds in the normal way. A cast is selected and it is decided how many rehearsals will be needed. Obviously the amount of time set aside for this will depend on the nature of the work that has been chosen, but a rough average works out at about a month's rehearsal.

With the requirements of the new production fixed it now remains for them to be fitted into the daily work of the opera house. This will involve setting up complicated timetables, some dealing with ordinary routine and others with the special needs of the new productions.

The soloists, meanwhile, are busy learning their parts from the opera's *Vocal Score*—that is to say, an arrangement of the music for voice and piano. To begin with they rehearse in sound-proofed rooms tucked away in various parts of the opera house or its outside buildings. These rooms contain a piano and the soloist's best friend, the repetiteur, whose task it is to play through the music and generally coach the singer in his part. The repetiteur acts as orchestra, conductor, producer and critic all rolled into one and is thus, at this stage, a key figure in preparing the opera.

While the singers are busy learning their parts the producer is occupied with the problem of presenting the opera on the stage. First he plans the broad outlines, using as his starting-point such indications as may be suggested by the music and the words. If a character sings about the 'fearful tempest and howling gale' or the music itself paints such a picture the producer is going to look foolish, to say the least, if he has set the stage to look like a sunny afternoon. Apart from such obvious requirements most operas can be interpreted with a reasonable degree of flexibility and it is within these limits that the producer will begin to show his own particular style and personality. But he will always bear in mind what the music is saying—for, as we have seen, it is the composer who is the dramatist and his conception must be obeyed. Nowadays most producers are careful to make their productions harmonize with the general spirit of an opera. Mozart, for example, calls for a completely different treatment from Wagner, and a work by Verdi calls for yet another approach. If this is misunderstood the result can ruin the greatest masterpiece.

In this respect the work of the stage designer is also of the greatest importance, for a sensitive stage-picture can set an atmosphere as soon as the curtain has risen. The designer will, of course, work in close co-operation with the producer, not only so as to avoid any conflict of style, but to ensure that the physical details of the stage set are all practical and suited to the needs of the production. The designer may have brilliant ideas for a scene, but the sets will be useless if they take up three-quarters of the stage and leave no room for the chorus. Nor is a set much use if it cannot be changed quickly between scenes—at the first performance of Sullivan's *Ivanhoe* one of the sets, a burning castle, was so realistic that the curtain had to be lowered for an unscheduled twenty minutes while the débris was cleared away!

Preparing the Opera

The designer must even be on his guard against being too clever and providing too many eye-catching spectacles, lest he only succeed in drawing away the audience's attention from the music. A brilliant stage set full of ingenious mechanical devices can spoil a work simply because it sets an audience wondering 'how it was done'.

The same kind of principles apply in designing the costumes. They must harmonize with the stage set, agree with any historical details in the opera's story and, most important of all, must underline the personality of each character. At the same time they must be easy to wear and effective to look at, even if they are made from the simplest materials.

Once these details have been settled, plans and sketches are passed to carpenters and scene-painters, costume- and wig-makers. In turn, these craftsmen fit the new task into their daily routine of refurbishing old sets, cleaning and repairing costumes and wigs, and so on.

At this stage most producers will have small models of the various sets for their own use, so that they can get an accurate idea of the production they are preparing. It is at this point that the most difficult part of his job begins. When he brings on a character he must know how to get him off again, how to get him to a certain point on the stage so that he may speak to another character, and so on. And all this must be done with a scrupulous regard for the music, for it is the music that controls the timing of each gesture, each apparent change of thought, each twist in the drama.

Two special problems arise in the production of opera that never occur in the ordinary theatre. In the first place operas contain many extended musical set-pieces (arias, duets and ensembles) all of which have the effect of slowing up the dramatic action. The producer must decide whether he can leave the music to absorb all the audience's attention or whether he must add stage 'business'—things for the characters to do while they are singing. The decision can often be extremely difficult to make, for the producer must balance the risk of boring his audience against the risk of annoying them with distracting by-play. The nearest the ordinary theatrical producer comes to this problem is when dealing with the long passages of poetry in Shakespeare's plays.

The other problem is that singers cannot easily cope with difficult physical movements. If they are to sing well there is no point in expecting them to rush about the stage or do athletic tricks on the scenery. Again, they must always, or nearly always, be in a position where they can pick up the conductor's beat whenever they need it (this is not to say that they will go through the entire performance with their eyes glued to the end of his baton; an occasional glance will be enough to keep them on the right lines).

Thus, the producer and stage designer work under certain limitations due to the nature of opera itself, and these limitations must be taken into account if a work is to have any chance of success on its own terms.

Once the singers have learned their parts and the producer has fixed the details of his production the Production Rehearsals will begin. These are carried out in everyday clothes to the accompaniment of a piano. There will be no scenery, perhaps not even a stage; simply a rehearsal room with chalk marks on the floor to show the size of the stage and the position of the imaginary scenery and furnishings. In this bleak setting the producer will start to instruct his cast in all the actions he has decided upon, so that they learn to blend them into the rhythm and mood of the music. Extraordinary care must be taken at this point, for action on the stage must fit the music as well as appear natural to the audience. A character who tries to match a soft lyrical phrase with a rough ungainly movement instantly spoils the illusion.

During the production rehearsals certain special 'props' are introduced (things like swords and goblets) so that the singers can learn to handle them without thinking. Often, the ladies will be asked to wear crinoline hoops so that no one will forget how far these dresses stick out. With their legs thus encased in bird-cages they make a comical addition to the rehearsal.

Once these preliminaries have begun to take shape the conductor will make a start with orchestral rehearsals. At Covent Garden the members of the orchestra are engaged on a basis of nine performances or rehearsals a week. Further rehearsals cost extra money and are therefore not to be encouraged. The orchestral rehearsals take place in the morning and last for three hours, so every effort is made to use them to the best advantage.

In the meantime the carpenters and painters will have completed the stage sets and the producer will call for stage rehearsals so that the stage-hands can get used to handling the scenery quickly and silently. He will then go through the entire work with the chief electrician, arranging the lighting for each scene and fixing the precise moment in relation to the music when each special effect is to be introduced.

At length, when singers and orchestra, stage-hands and electricians all know the part they must play, the final dress rehearsal is called and the opera is performed to an empty theatre. Last-minute adjustments are made and everything is ready for the first public performance.

The Ingredients of Opera

But the work of the opera house goes on. There are new operas to be prepared and old ones to tidy up. Once a work has entered the repertory it is only rehearsed again if it has not been performed for more than six months, or if there have been important changes in the cast. However, singers may ask for advice and private coaching in a part that causes them concern. So too may a conductor or chorus master find time during his weekly schedule of rehearsals to pick up a point that the previous night's performance has revealed. Routine tasks, like checking the lighting equipment and the stage machinery, touching up damaged sets and cleaning soiled costumes, continue as a matter of course. Cleaners descend on the empty theatre and barmen restock with drinks and refreshments. There is scarcely a moment's lull in the multifarious activities of an opera house. No wonder, then, that a General Administrator will tell you that his job requires the strategy of a Field-Marshal and the foresight of a crystal-gazer.

PART TWO
An Outline of Operatic History

VII

Opera in the Seventeenth Century

MOST accounts of operatic history begin at about the year 1600, for it was at this time that the first operas came into existence. But it would be wrong to let the convenience of a nice round date blind one to the fact that these early operas had many forerunners. Indeed, the use of music in the theatre, which, after all, is what opera amounts to, has a long and honourable history.

The most primitive forms of drama are the religious ceremonies that man evolved for himself far back in the beginnings of his history. It seems likely that music, in the form of singing, clapping hands and beating drums, played an important part in these ceremonies, particularly as an accompaniment to ritual dances. Even today music plays its part in religious ceremony and helps to lift the believer on to a higher emotional plane. How much more effective it must have been when its use was confined to these ceremonial occasions can only be guessed at. But it is hardly surprising to find that in ancient times music was thought to have magical powers.

In the earliest recorded plays, those of the ancient Greeks, we find that music is still closely associated with drama, even though the drama itself has developed far beyond religious ritual. It seems likely that large parts of these plays were sung or chanted by a chorus; though, since none of the music has come down to us, we cannot tell precisely how it was done or what it sounded like. Oddly enough it was the imperfect understanding of the part music played in Greek drama that gave birth to modern opera at the end of the sixteenth century.

The drama and musical drama of Western civilization, however, owes its rebirth to the ceremonial of the Christian Church and not, as is sometimes suggested, to Greek tragedy. When the Graeco-Roman civilizations collapsed their forms of drama vanished too, and it was not until the tenth century of Christian civilization that the seeds of a new dramatic art were sown. And they were very small seeds indeed.

At this period the music of the Christian Church consisted mainly of Chants, whose tunes had been gathered together from many different sources, Greek and Jewish among them, and were eventually codified by Pope Gregory I around the year 600. Although this body of *Gregorian Chant* came to be regarded as having the same sort of religious value as the words of the Bible itself, the tunes were none the less open to variation and addition and there soon arose a practice known as *troping*. Tropes were simply bits added to the official chant. For example: 'Kyrie Eleison' (Lord, have mercy) might be expanded to become 'Kyrie Deus sempiterne eleison' (Lord, everlasting God, have mercy). The melody of the chant was tretched out to fit the new words.

In the tenth century somebody added a trope to the Introit (Psalm) that was sung as part of the Easter Mass. This trope consisted of a dialogue between the three Marys and an Angel, who meet outside the tomb of Christ. The angel asks:

'Whom do ye seek in the tomb, O servants of Christ?'

and the women answer:

'Jesus of Nazareth who was crucified, O celestial one.'

It is from this tiny scrap of dialogue that the whole of Western drama springs; for soon other scenes were added, covering all the important events in the life of Christ, and gradually costumes and dramatic action were introduced. Music, however, slipped to one side when the drama began to develop, but was still brought in to heighten the emotional effect wherever necessary.

The Church realized that in these tiny dramas it had an excellent means of impressing the main facts of the Bible on the minds of people who could not read. Unfortunately the dramas became so popular that they rather overstepped the mark and became increasingly an entertainment, so that in 1207 Pope Innocent III was forced to pass an act forbidding performances inside the church. After this the church dramas were taken over by professional actors, and the stage, originally set up in the nave or on the church steps, was transferred to the market place. This later form of church drama led to the Mystery and Miracle Plays sponsored by the various Guilds of the fifteenth and sixteenth centuries and these, as we know, are the direct forerunners of modern European drama.

It is interesting to note that one of the reasons for Pope Innocent's edict against the church dramas was that not only had they become spectacular and had begun to drop the use of Latin in favour of the local tongue, but that musically they had abandoned Gregorian Chant in favour of popular tunes. In all essentials they had become Church Operas.

Opera as we know it ought, therefore, to have sprung from these roots; but in the direct sense it did not. Rather, music retreated into second place as something to be used to increase an emotional effect, or conjure up a sense of mystery (angels, for example, tended to sing); while drama and its own music (the music of poetry) took the foremost position. And when, eventually, opera did come into existence it did so as the result of entirely different considerations.

The inventors of modern opera were members of one of the many intellectual clubs that had sprung up all over Italy during the late Renaissance. The members of these clubs were accustomed to meet from time to time and discuss the problems of art and science. The particular group that gave birth to the idea of opera was founded in Florence about the year 1580. They called themselves the *Camerata*. Among the members was the nobleman Count Bardi, at whose palace their meetings first took place, the poet Rinuccini and the composers Jacopo Peri, Emilio de' Cavalieri and Vincenzo Galilei.

It was Galilei, the son of the great astronomer, who began the whole affair by publishing, in 1581, a pamphlet in which he attacked the elaborate contrapuntal style of the Renaissance (the style of Palestrina), declaring that it was incapable of expressing words clearly because the various melodic lines sooner or later contradicted each other. He argued that it should be replaced by a 'new music' consisting of a single melodic line which imitated the natural rise and fall of speech and which was to be supported by a series of simple chords played on some instrument.

Galilei's friends took up the challenge and began to

experiment with the 'new music' under the happy, though mistaken idea that they were reviving the practice of ancient Greek drama. It must here be emphasized that the men of the Renaissance looked to Greek culture as a source of inspiration.

However, the contrapuntal style was too strong to be overthrown just like that and after a few rather dull experiments the 'new music' began to take over some of the old features. The melodies themselves became more subtle and expressive, forgetting the rather limited 'natural rise and fall' of speech; and though the accompanying harmonies were still thought of as blocks of sound a certain interest in part writing began to return.

The important fact is that opera came about as part of a general desire to express emotion in terms of music. The word 'opera' itself was not used in the modern sense until the end of the seventeenth century. The early composers described their works as 'Dramas in Music', which suggests that they considered the words as rather more important than the music. The first of these works seems to have been the *Dafne* which Jacopo Peri composed in 1597 to a libretto by Rinuccini. The music, however, has since been lost; but another work, *The Representation of the Soul and the Body* by Cavalieri, which was produced in 1600, has survived intact and thus qualifies as the first opera. Although it deals with a semi-religious subject Cavalieri's work is a true opera and consists of solos written in the new monodic style (the style of the 'new music') interspersed with simple choruses, dances and interludes. The whole thing is accompanied by an orchestra.

The first opera on a completely secular subject is Peri's *Euridice* which was also produced in 1600, as part of the celebrations that accompanied the marriage of Henry IV of France to Marie de' Medici. Shortly afterwards Caccini made a setting of the same words, but this was not produced until 1602. Thus it is fair to say that by the end of 1600 opera was no longer a matter of theory but an aesthetic fact.

The idea soon spread beyond Florence. However, it must be admitted that only one of the many composers who took up the problem in its early stages had anything of the overwhelming genius needed to provide a truly artistic solution. This man was Claudio Monteverdi (1567–1643).

Monteverdi produced his first opera, *Orfeo*, at Mantua in 1607. Instead of relying solely upon the rather limited monodic style that had served Peri and his friends he introduced elements from all the styles available at the time. The monodic style appears side by side with shapely songs; choruses in block harmony are matched by choruses in madrigal style; instrumental interludes are used throughout to bind the different elements of each scene together and give it musical shape. The entire work is scored for a large and colourful orchestra.

Perhaps the most remarkable thing about Monteverdi's music is his extraordinary ability to capture emotions in terms of musical phrases and striking harmonies. He was one of the first composers to realize that the colours of individual harmonies might be made to represent a dramatic idea, and he exploited this discovery with consummate skill. His music fits the drama like a glove.

Altogether Monteverdi wrote twenty-one dramatic works, but only six have survived. Of this number the three operas alone—*Orfeo*, 1607, *The Return of Ulysses*, 1641 and *The Coronation of Poppea*, 1642—are enough to tell us that the loss of the others is one of the major tragedies in the history of music and that beyond any doubt Monteverdi was not only the first great operatic composer, but one of the greatest composers of all time.

In 1637 the first public opera house was opened in Venice and the business of opera passed from the exclusive patronage of noblemen to the whims of the general public. During the next fifty years eleven more theatres were opened in Venice alone. Composers such as Monteverdi (who moved to Venice in 1614), Cavalli (1602–76), Cesti (1623–69) and Legrenzi (1626–90) became popular favourites and their works soon spread to the courts of France and Germany, helping, as we shall see, to establish Italian opera on foreign soil.

The importance of public opera houses cannot be overestimated, for the taste of the man in the street, whose patronage was now being sought, has scarcely ever been on the highest level. As a result opera began to undergo considerable changes. The tunes became simpler; rhythms became more obvious and dance-like; harmonies tended to centre round the major and minor modes. This process of simplification eventually led to the establishment of formal patterns in music—clear-cut principles of Statement, Contrast and Repetition—and it was these that were to have a most important bearing on the later development of orchestral and chamber music.

While these features were valuable in themselves they were paralleled by less fortunate developments. Spectacular changes of scenery became the order of the day. The standards of characterisation and dramatic logic in the librettos began to decline (though partly because this was a period of literary poverty in Italy). The simple melodic style gradually gave way to vocal acrobatics. Within a short time the principles that had inspired the *Camerata* degenerated into meaningless entertainment.

This collapse of ideals in no way hindered the popularity of opera. Not only did it spread throughout Italy, establishing particularly important centres in Naples and Rome, but it found its way into the rest of Europe. Austria, South Germany and Bohemia seem to have been the first countries to import Italian opera, with North Germany and France following soon after. Only France, however, had sufficient vitality to create a national style of her own—ironically, through the genius of an Italian, Jean Baptiste Lully (1632–87), who lived in Paris from the age of ten and was to all intents and purposes a Frenchman. By the judicious and almost wholly unscrupulous exercise of his influence over King Louis XIV Lully obtained complete control over all operatic ventures in France and thereupon proceeded to saturate the theatres with his own works. Fortunately his genius equalled his lack of modesty and he created a style of operatic composition which was to have a permanent effect on French opera.

In simple terms an opera by Lully differs from the typical Italian opera of the same period in that the libretto is as important as the music. The stories are therefore less absurd. Moreover, there are fewer arias and these are simpler and more dignified in style than their Italian counterparts. The recitatives are important in themselves and are not just a convenient link between arias. There are more choruses and Ballet plays an important part. The orchestra too plays a larger part in the Lully opera, acting not only as an accompaniment to the voices, but on its own account through the various dances and interludes and, most of all, the Overture.

The whole point of a Lully opera, however, was to glorify the King and the idea of monarchy. Everything in the opera underlined this point, and thus, to a large extent, real passion and emotion had to be avoided. Whatever the story might be it had somehow to be bent round to accommodate flattering references to the King. Yet Lully managed to turn even this to good account. The spectacular ballets and grandiose choruses in which gods and goddesses hailed the magnificence of the Sun King all helped to give his work a monumental grandeur. And this, coupled with the fact that his librettos were works of distinct literary merit (this, after all, was the France of Molière, Racine and Corneille), and the fact that he set words with scrupulous care, puts his work in line with the traditions of Monteverdi and the *Camerata*.

Towards the end of the seventeenth century the centre of the Italian opera industry, for this is what it had become, moved to Naples where, in the works of Alessandro Scarlatti (1660–1725), Italian opera took on its typical eighteenth-century form.

Unfortunately it chose to sacrifice dramatic sense to the delights of musical variety. The plots, such as they were, were disposed of quickly by means of recitative. This came in two grades: a simple kind, *recitativo secco*, which was a quick musical patter accompanied by a few chords on the harpsichord and which served very well for ordinary matter-of-fact remarks; and a more elaborate style known as accompanied recitative, *recitativo stromentato*, which was accompanied by the orchestra and was used for more emotional statements. These recitatives served as a link between the really important parts of the opera: the arias, which were supposed to reveal the emotions of the chief characters. Variety was achieved by arranging that successive arias should present different emotions. This was especially necessary because convention also demanded that no aria might present more than one emotion at a time. Thus, there arose many different types of aria: the agitated *Aria di bravura*, for excited emotions, the lyrical *Aria cantabile* for sentiment, the slow-moving *Aria di portamento* for dignified moods, and so on.

The distribution of arias throughout the opera was also controlled. Generally each scene ended with an aria, and each member of the cast expected at least one aria in each of the opera's three acts. However, no performer might have two arias one after the other, nor might two arias expressing the same mood follow one another. The most important arias, sung by the most important characters, had to come at the end of the first and second acts. In the second and third acts the two leading singers expected a 'grand scena' apiece—each consisting of an accompanied recitative followed by a virtuoso display aria. The hero and heroine also expected at least one grand duet and, since most operas were made to end happily whatever else happened, all the surviving characters rounded off the third act with a rousing ensemble.

Though the arias might differ in mood they were all similar in form, consisting of a main tune, a contrast, and a restatement of the main tune with vocal decorations added. This formal pattern became known as the *Aria da Capo*. The basic mood of each aria was established very firmly by means of an orchestral introduction which announced a 'motto theme'—that is: a bold musical idea which pinpoints the mood. Since the opening words also made use of this phrase there was never any doubt as to the meaning of each aria.

Alongside the *Aria da Capo* there grew up a whole tribe of virtuoso singers. The accepted number for each opera was six: three women and three men. The leading woman was always a high Soprano, while the other two had lower voices—one at least being a Contralto. In practice the Contralto might easily be expected to take the part of a man. As for the three men: the leading man was always a Castrato, the second either a Castrato or an Alto, and the third was a true Tenor. If, as sometimes happened, a fourth man was needed his was usually a Bass voice. However, such was the popularity of the Castrati that they might even take over the women's parts, so that the entire opera would be sung by men of one shade of voice or another.

Thus the eighteenth-century opera was a vehicle for the solo singer, while the composer and librettist limped along some way behind simply as agents in glorifying the singer's vanity. However, it must be admitted that many singers were musicians of taste and skill. Such was their ability that they could transform the average minor composer's work into something far above its real worth. All we have left are the bare notes—we have to imagine the glory that the great singer could cast over them.

And it was this, in a sense, that was the root of the weakness in eighteenth-century opera. The singers dominated everybody. Composers were in no position to deny them what they wanted: more and more arias to show off their voices. A few men, like Scarlatti and Handel, still managed to produce work that satisfied the singers and yet remained artistically worth while, but they were in the minority. In general the standard of composition was low and the demand for new music unending. Composers were forced to drum up 'new' operas from bits and pieces of older works in a feverish endeavour to satisfy the market. In this way the general run of Italian opera soon fell into mediocrity and total disrepute.

VIII

Handel and the Eighteenth Century

THE Italian opera of the early eighteenth century was saved from complete absurdity by the influence of two poets whose libretti became so popular that they were set over and over again by composers of all countries throughout the century. Although these two men, Apostolo Zeno (1668–1750) and Pietro Metastasio (1698–1782), were largely responsible for the conventional form that opera took, they still managed to warm the conventions with imaginative touches and a degree of poetry which, if it reached no great heights, was at least eminently suited to musical setting. Moreover, they ensured that the convention they perfected was carried out consistently. They accepted conditions as they found them, but tidied up the loose ends and cleared away the most glaring absurdities.

Meanwhile, Italian opera spread throughout Europe. A native German opera struggled for a while in Hamburg, but, despite composers of genuine ability like Reinhard Keiser (1674–1739), soon fell to the Italian style. English opera, as we shall see, made a promising start only to be swept away after the death of Purcell. French opera alone had firm enough roots to withstand the invasion and was fortunate enough to find a successor to Lully in Jean-Philippe Rameau (1683–1764).

Rameau first came into prominence as a theorist and only turned to opera when he was fifty. Generally speaking, his operas are in the traditions of Lully, with considerable emphasis on spectacular scenery, elaborate ballets and impressive choruses. His arias, however, are more Italianate than Lully's—that is to say, they are more graceful and sensuous. Rameau's weak point was his willingness to accept second-rate libretti in an attempt to satisfy the enormous demand there was for his work. A true child of the French 'age of reason', which saw salvation in a back-to-nature philosophy, he was also the first composer to make any considerable use of the orchestra for descriptive purposes. His operas abound in stormy seas, approaching thunderstorms and the like; all of which helped to underline the spectacular side of French opera. Considering how great Rameau's purely musical gifts were it is all the more unfortunate that his literary taste was so haphazard. Had he been more concerned with dramatic common sense his operas might well have challenged the supremacy of Italian opera in Europe.

And that Italian opera *was* supreme there can be no doubt. Even the greatest operatic composer of the time, George Frederick Handel (1685–1750), was a composer of opera in the Italian style. Although his first stage works were written in German for Hamburg he found himself drawn to the music of Italy. He spent three years there and soon learned everything the Italians could teach him and by 1709, when *Agrippina* was produced in Venice, he was openly acknowledged as the equal of any Italian composer. Henceforth he was known to them as 'il caro sassone'.

But Handel was too shrewd a businessman to remain in

Italy. He saw that London was eager for Italian opera and had no native composer worthy of consideration. He took up residence and in 1711 scored an immediate success with *Rinaldo*. From that moment his career was a long succession of brilliant musical triumphs bedevilled by operatic intrigue. A series of financial disasters eventually brought him to a standstill and he composed his last opera, *Deidamia*, in 1741. Within a fortnight of its failure Handel began work on the *Messiah* and from then on concentrated all his efforts on establishing Oratorio—itself, although the English scarcely like to admit as much, a form of opera.

Despite the religious trappings, the biblical heroes and Old Testament stories, the Handel oratorio has much in common with the Handel opera. Musically the style is the same—the major difference lying in the extensive use the oratorios make of the chorus, which, as we have seen, scarcely existed in Italian opera. Even in this Handel showed his remarkable business instincts, for nothing was more likely to appeal to English tastes and English traditions than bold, massive choral effects.

It is unfortunate that until comparatively recently Handel the composer of oratorio has rather overshadowed Handel the supreme master of early eighteenth-century opera. His great strength lay in his remarkable melodic gifts, which seized upon ordinary materials and immediately transformed them into something individual and memorable. An aria like 'Where ere you walk', from *Semele*, is typical of the hundreds of equally beautiful melodies which crowd his forty-odd operas. Serene and expressive, admirably suited to the human voice, instantly memorable, it explains why he was able to conquer London in so short a time. Moreover, his creative abilities were sufficient to enable him to overcome the limitations of eighteenth-century operatic convention and create, in his greatest works (such as *Julius Caesar*) characters that are not just dumb pegs for arias, but convincing in flesh-and-blood terms.

Though Italy gave Handel the broad basis of his style, with its sweeping melodic lines and bold diatonic harmonies, he learned from France to delight in orchestral richness, and from Germany to reinforce his persuasive melodies with carefully wrought textures. His craftsmanship was thus formidable, and since it was called into service by a highly original natural genius the effect was inevitably overwhelming. He stands, even today, alongside the greatest operatic masters of all time.

One of the contributing factors to Handel's ultimate financial collapse was the sudden rise in popularity of comic opera—in particular, John Gay's ballad opera of 1728: *The Beggar's Opera*. This work, and its successors, will be dealt with in a later chapter and it is sufficient now simply to note its existence as part of a general tendency which swept through the operatic stages of Europe during this period. However much an eighteenth-century audience might delight in fine singing it was hardly to be expected that it would go on suffering the ludicrous aspects of Italian opera in silence. The stiff formalities were ripe for a little mockery and the mocking laughter came in the form of comic opera.

In Italy the comic style of opera was known as the *Opera buffa*. Its origins go back to the seventeenth-century practice of introducing comic episodes in the middle of serious operas. Gradually these episodes took on a life of their own and grew away from the parent opera, soon becoming everything that serious opera was not and could not be. Plots were humorous and life-like, characters natural and human. Recitatives ran smoothly and swiftly, arias were short and lively and shorn of all complication. The whole tone of *opera buffa* was casual, conversational and realistic.

Perhaps the most delightful of the *opera buffa* composers was Giovanni Pergolesi (1710–36), whose *La Serva Padrona* is still performed to this day. While in the hands of such composers as Piccinni (1728–1800), Paisiello (1740–1816), and Cimarosa (1769–1801), the form developed into a highly organized alternative to serious opera.

Nor was its influence confined to Italy. In France the spirit of laughter blossomed as the *Opéra-comique*, in Germany as the *Singspiel*, and in England as the *Ballad opera*. In one respect these three countries went one stage further than Italy, for they dropped recitative altogether and linked the songs by spoken dialogue. But in other respects they had much in common—simple melodies, a natural approach, and stories that were more or less realistic. In France the *Opéra-comique* found admirable composers in Philidor (1726–95), Monsigny (1729–1817), and Grétry (1742–1813). English *Ballad opera* thrived in the hands of Arne (1710–78), Dibdin (1745–1814), Shield (1748–1829) and Storace (1763–96). It was left to Germany, however, to produce the supreme master of the *buffa* style—Wolfgang Amadeus Mozart.

Whereas serious opera suited the tastes of the aristocracy, comic opera reflected the tastes of the man in the street. Ultimately it forced serious opera to laugh at its own absurdities and mend its ways by advancing to a position where it could once more become a means of expressing genuine human emotion.

IX

Gluck and Mozart

THE rise of comic opera is only one symptom of a general change of attitude in the second half of the eighteenth century. Little by little the intellectual and artistic atmosphere of Western Europe was beginning to alter, breaking away from artificial formal convention, away from rationalist philosophy and moving towards a delight in the natural, unaffected expression of human feelings. In terms of philosophy the great prophet of this movement was Jean-Jacques Rousseau (1712–78), himself an enthusiastic, if rather amateurish, composer. His ideal of man as the 'noble savage', born free yet everywhere in chains, had far-reaching effects both on politics and art, helping to generate an enthusiasm for self-expression that led on the one hand to the French Revolution and on the other to the Romantic Movement of the early nineteenth century.

In its early stages, however, Rousseau's philosophy was tempered by other notions of a less explosive nature—in particular yet another rediscovery of the glories of ancient Greece, this time as revealed by the findings of a German archaeologist, Johann Winckleman, who published his remarkable *History of Ancient Art* in 1764. Winckleman argued that the lesson Greek art was 'noble simplicity and calm greatness', and this motto might well serve as a description of that period of European art which we now call 'Classical' (in music the period of Haydn, Mozart and Beethoven). The two composers who, in their different ways, sum up the operatic harvest of these new ideas are Christoph Willibald Gluck (1714–98) and Wolfgang Amadeus Mozart (1756–91).

Gluck was born in Bohemia, the son of a peasant. The only certain details of his musical education are that in 1736, after spending several years in Prague and Vienna, he was sent by a noble patron to study with the composer Sammartini in Milan. His first operas were produced in Italy between the years 1741 and 1745. There is little to distinguish them from the average Italian opera of the period. In 1745 he visited London and there produced two rather unsuccessful operas and made the acquaintance of Handel and his music. In later years Gluck told Dr. Charles Burney that this had been the 'turning-point' in his career, and it is possible that by this he meant that Handel's oratorios had had some influence on him. During the next few years, however, he travelled extensively in Europe, spending most of his time in Vienna and Paris and producing operas both in Italian and French.

Had his career remained on this level he would by now have been completely forgotten, but in 1762 he produced a work which not only revolutionized his career but had a profound effect on opera in general. That his intention was to reform opera can hardly be doubted. The new work, *Orfeo*, was based on the same subject that had inspired the early Florentine composers and which, in turn, had been used by Monteverdi as the subject of his first operatic masterpiece. Both the composer and his librettist, Calzibigi, were influenced by current intellectual ideas, particularly those of the Italian philosopher Algarotti, who advocated a change in the attitude to opera that amounted to nothing less than a complete revolt against the principles of Metastasio. Calzibigi seems to have been the prime mover in this campaign of reform, and indeed Gluck wrote:

If my music has had some success I think it my duty to recognize that I am beholden for it to him, since it was he who enabled me to develop the resources of my art.

Calzibigi himself was even more enthusiastic about the part he had played.

Apart from two conventional features—the overture and the artificial happy ending—*Orfeo* is very different from the ordinary Italian opera of the period. In it action is cut to a minimum, so that the drama can develop through the spiritual growth of the characters themselves. The music, like the libretto, is simple and without ornamentation. Its aim is to express emotion rather than pander to the vanity of singers and the stupidity of audiences. The *da capo* aria is abandoned in favour of simpler and less predictable forms. The recitative is always accompanied by the orchestra, so there is less of a break between it and the arias. And over all there is a feeling of classical grandeur— noble simplicity and calm greatness.

Further 'reform' operas followed. In 1767 Gluck and Calzibigi collaborated on *Alceste*, again choosing a Greek legend. This was followed by *Paride ed Elena* in 1770, *Iphigénie en Aulide* in 1774, *Armide* in 1777, and *Iphigénie en Tauride* in 1779—the last three being written for Paris. The interest in all these operas centres upon the workings of the human mind in difficult situations, rather than the mechanical working out of a 'plot'. Gluck's characters have a vitality and human interest that lift them far above the general run of opera. In his hands opera again became drama, and it is not surprising to find that his works are among the earliest that still have a place in the general repertory.

It would, however, be wrong to assume that simply because they were different from the normal eighteenth-century ideal Gluck's operas necessarily prove that this ideal was itself incapable of greatness. In the hands of a composer of genius it too could be transformed into a thing of lasting beauty and significance.

That this was so is amply borne out by the career of Mozart. He was never a conscious 'reformer', the idea of reforming anybody or anything would probably never have occurred to him; but his genius was such that he invariably transformed everything he touched. Mozart's early career is probably too well known to need repetition here, but it is important to recognize that in being exhibited through-out the major countries of Europe as an infant prodigy he had an unrivalled opportunity to learn, at first hand, the different styles these countries had bred. Few composers have had so thorough a musical education.

To begin with, of course, the young Mozart tried out current operatic manners for himself. His first opera, *La Finta Semplice*, written when he was only twelve, is a conventional *buffo* piece in the style of Pergolesi and his contemporaries. Shortly afterwards he produced *Bastien and Bastienne*, a work obviously modelled on the *Opéra-comique* style of France. *Mitradate* and *Lucio Silla*, which date from 1770 and 1772, are exercises in the Italian *opera seria* manner. And so he continued, learning and experimenting, until he arrived at his first important operatic commission as a mature composer. The opera he produced in 1780, *Idomeneo*, is the only one which shows any trace of Gluck's influence. The libretto itself is of the old-fashioned Metastasian variety and, appropriately, Mozart provided it with many brilliant arias in the Italian style; but the choruses, orchestral interludes and accompanied recitatives are modelled on Gluck. One feature, however, is peculiar to Mozart, and that is to be found in the great quartet in the third act. Here Mozart expresses the conflicting emotions of the four main characters, showing them both as individuals and in their relationship to one another and the situation in general. Musically they are clearly individuals, yet the four threads combine to give an overall unity. This ability to reveal the interplay of conflicting character in terms of music is, as we shall see, the thing that ultimately raises Mozart's opera head and shoulders above those of his contemporaries. Scarlatti, Rameau and Handel had attempted something of the sort, but their achievements pale beside his solution to the problem.

But although Mozart's genius gave new life to the *opera seria* the convention was in decline and, apart from the ill-fated *La Clemenza di Tito* of 1791, he himself wrote nothing more in this style. *Idomeneo* is thus one of the last of the species.

Already, then, it is possible to point the difference between Mozart's contribution to opera and that of Gluck. For Gluck the reform of opera was a conscious thing—he even claimed that when he composed he tried to forget he was a musician. To him music was simply the means through which the drama achieved its fullest expression. His music appeals less to the senses than to the rational mind and thus he may well have meant more to an eighteenth-century audience, who set great store by the idea of 'rational man', than he does to us, who find the appeal rather austere.

Mozart, however, was no more a conscious philosopher

than Shakespeare. His understanding of human nature was as instinctive as his ability to translate this understanding into music. His characters are therefore completely human. They do not represent one particular quality, as do Gluck's; but, like all human beings, are a mixture of good and bad, noble and base, all inextricably mingled and constantly changing. Thus they are as alive today as they were when Mozart first created them and will, without doubt, continue to live.

Mozart's next opera, *Die Entführung aus dem Serail*, was written in 1782 for the new *Singspiel* theatre in Vienna which the Emperor Joseph II had created to replace the old Italian opera which he had just abolished in a fit of enthusiasm for purely national art. Mozart's opera, however, is not just the routine formula of simple, folk-like tunes that served most *Singspiel*. *Die Entführung* mixes several styles—simple tunes, brilliant *buffo* songs, elaborate arias in the serious Italian style, and picturesque 'Turkish' music thrown in for good measure. On the whole the mixture is not quite convincing, though, as we shall see, the instinct that prompted him to attempt the feat was sound enough.

It was not until four years later, in 1786, that Mozart produced the first of his great operatic masterpieces, *The Marriage of Figaro*. This time he had the services of Lorenzo da Ponte, a librettist, who, if not a man of genius in his own right, was at least able to supply intelligent work written with an acute appreciation of Mozart's needs. The characters in the opera are stock types, but da Ponte's libretto left room for Mozart to transcend the conventions. The work thus remains within the traditions of *opera buffa*, but the elements of that tradition are thoroughly revitalized.

Gluck and Mozart

The major reason for this rebirth lies in the fact that the dramatic action, as expressed in Mozart's music, now revolves round the conflict between distinct personalities. Significantly, the number of arias is greatly reduced in favour of *ensembles*. The characters are constantly in conversation with one another, each acting upon the other's individuality. Thus the action is never held up, for the characters develop within the musical set-pieces.

The Marriage of Figaro enjoyed only a brief success in Vienna, but met with a more appreciative audience in Prague where enthusiasm took the practical form of a commission for a new opera. Mozart and da Ponte met the challenge with *Don Giovanni* (1787). They called the work a 'dramma giocosa', which suggests that they were well aware it fitted neither into the traditions of *opera seria*, or of *opera buffa*. Musically it borrowed from both styles: the chattering *buffo* patter of Leporello's arias, the sepulchral trombones of *opera seria* that accompany the dead Commendatore, the lighthearted frivolity of Don Giovanni, and the heart-rending tragedy of Donna Elvira. But Mozart had developed considerably since *Die Entführung* and the opposing styles now blend perfectly.

Although there are as many ensembles in *Don Giovanni* as there are in *The Marriage of Figaro*, it is the arias that set the tone and stamp the personality of each character on the mind. They are, however, shorter than most eighteenth-century arias, and, since they are all addressed to some other person on the stage, never appear to hold up the action. The *ensembles* are less important because the characters are not so inextricably mixed up with each other as they are in *Figaro*. Indeed, Don Giovanni is the only one who is involved with everyone else and the *ensembles* are mainly interesting for the light they throw on his character.

And what a remarkable character it is! Don Giovanni is both villain and tragic hero, seen through the spectacles of a comedy that is by turns cynical, indulgent and always wise.

Cosi van Tutti, Mozart's next opera, was also the last for which da Ponte wrote the libretto. It is a masterpiece of artificial comedy and represents the high-water mark of the Italian *opera buffa*. The story, with its two pairs of lovers and inevitable trail of mistaken identities, has been described as 'the apotheosis of insincerity'. The music might equally well be called 'the apotheosis of the ensemble', for here Mozart's command of the art of musical conversation reaches supreme heights.

Mozart's last opera, *Die Zauberflöte*, proved to be his masterpiece. It is not easy to write about, for although on the surface it seems little more than a preposterous fairy-tale it becomes, by virtue of Mozart's music, a deeply serious morality. The libretto is an extraordinary jumble, the work of Emanuel Schikaneder, an actor-manager who was in charge of the *Theatre auf der Wieden* which specialized in spectacular fairy-tale plays. Both Mozart and Schikaneder were Freemasons and they contrived to underpin what had started out as a simple fairy story with the liberal, and at this date subversive, ideals of their creed. The work may thus be regarded as having two levels: the level of comic entertainment, and the level of Masonic idealism.

Mozart's music adds a third and deeper level—that of his understanding of human nature. But we can only appreciate this when we learn to understand the meaning of his phrases as, delicately, they hint at the spiritual growth of his characters. As a revelation of the growth of two human souls to an acceptance of mature wisdom and responsibility *Die Zauberflöte* is without parallel in all opera. It is, in this sense, a deeply religious work.

It is also a work in which an extraordinary variety of different musical elements are blended into a convincing musical unity. Simple folk-like songs, such as might be found in any *Singspiel*, sit happily alongside elaborate coloratura arias of the old *opera seria* tradition. Music appropriate to a solemn masonic ceremony is followed by brilliant operatic ensembles. A Bach-like Chorale treated with all the resources of austere counterpoint, is balanced by phrases of tender sensuous passion. By all logical standards the work should entirely fail to make its point, but Mozart's genius somehow fuses the contradictions into an immortal masterpiece.

One aspect of Mozart's contribution to opera has yet to be mentioned: his handling of the orchestra. This, as might be expected of a great symphonic composer, is masterly and far removed from the general run of simple 'accompaniment' that serves most operas. Not only does his choice of instruments fit the scene he wishes to describe, but fits also the characters he is dealing with. The orchestral background is rich and varied, but never challenges the supremacy of the voice. It is ready, when needed, to share the burden of musical development; ready at times to reveal by its comments some truth that the characters may be concealing even from themselves. It is at once the unobtrusive means of support to the vocal line's revelation of character and an infinitely variable resource for deepening and enriching that revelation.

Mozart is, beyond doubt, one of the supreme dramatists of all time.

X

Opera in the Nineteenth Century

APART from the occasional contribution from France, the history of opera during the first two hundred years of its existence is virtually a history of the development of opera in the Italian style. During those two hundred years Italian opera mushroomed all over Europe. Italian singers sang Italian words that had been set to music by Italian composers and found no difficulty in giving delight to audiences for whom Italian was a foreign language. Composers from less fortunate countries found it advisable to learn Italian so that they might set the fashionable Italian libretti to music, and most of them made special efforts to travel in Italy and so gain first-hand knowledge of its music.

Now although it is undeniable that the Italian style reached great heights during this period, its popularity in foreign countries was mainly among the aristocracy, for whom it had a certain snob appeal. Only the various forms of comic opera can be said to have any national flavour, and this was precisely because they aimed at a lower class of audience and stuck, therefore, to the native language of the particular country. In a sense the eighteenth-century Italian opera is an international opera belonging to an exclusive upper class of all nations. Once the power of this aristocracy began to weaken, as it did at the time of the French Revolution, the more human ideals expressed so far only in comic opera began to come to the surface, bringing with them distinctly national flavours. It is as if the revolutionary cry of 'Liberty, Equality, Fraternity' that made ordinary people aware of their own equal importance as individuals also made the various nations aware of their own individuality. Opera, and all art, reflected this change of attitude. The old international style gave way to a number of different styles, each carrying the flavour of its own country. From this point it is no longer possible to concentrate on the history of one country's opera; each country has begun to develop its own style and has, therefore, its own special history.

It would, of course, be foolish to imagine nineteenth-century opera as being split up into watertight national compartments. The different national characteristics influenced each other and, indeed, followed basically similar patterns of development. The point is simply that each country now began to speak for itself, not only in its own language, but in the language of its own music.

This discovery of national individuality is very much in line with the general change of attitude that came over all art at the end of the eighteenth century. The typical eighteenth-century artist may be said to have been rather more concerned with the perfection of his craft than with the expression of personal emotion. Obviously his work *did* express his emotions, but it did so only incidentally. His whole attitude, and the attitude of his age, was such that to express extreme personal emotion would be a breach of manners. Emotion had its place—in a balanced, ordered whole. Not so the typical nineteenth-century artist. He had discovered his personal uniqueness and was determined on self-expression at all costs. For him each work was a page of autobiography, a revelation of his soul. It is therefore not surprising to find the art of the nineteenth century full of eccentricity and wild personal emotion. The eighteenth-century artist stuck to calm, well-ordered themes, and a style that we now call 'classical'; his nineteenth-century counterpart let his imagination take him where it would, and thus earned for himself the title: 'romantic'.

At the turn of the century the centre of operatic development moved, for a while, to France. Far from disrupting theatrical life the Revolution acted as a stimulus, encouraging, in particular, enormous public entertainments—national festivals culminating in vast choral hymns to be sung by the entire audience. These in turn encouraged a type of spectacular opera which eventually became known as *Grand Opera*.

Perhaps the most important composer of the revolutionary period in France was Luigi Cherubini (1760–1842)—yet another foreign Frenchman. His music, which often suggests the style of early Beethoven, stands half-way between classicism and romanticism. Despite such masterpieces as *Médée* (1797) which harks back to the austere manner of Gluck, his most important contribution to the development of opera came in the year 1800 with *Les Deux Journées*. This work helped to establish a new type of opera: the 'rescue opera', which depended on thrilling, last-minute escapes from some dreadful fate. Cherubini did not invent this type of opera, which dates back to about 1790, but his contribution is certainly one of the masterpieces of the kind—another is Beethoven's *Fidelio*. The topicality of such plots is obvious when one considers the events of the revolution.

Opera in the Nineteenth Century

Opera in the grand manner reached a climax, as one might expect, during Napoleon's First Empire, and in the works of his favourite composer Gaspare Spontini (1774–1851). His masterpiece, *La Vestale* (1807), managed to combine the elements of a rescue plot with a passionate love story, spectacular crowd scenes, an historical background and strong, melodramatic climaxes. On the whole the sensational aspects of his work are kept under control, so that it is still possible to see the influence of Gluck; but his massive choral set-pieces, and his delight in piling up thunderous orchestral climaxes, opened the way to all manner of abuses.

Ultimately *Grand Opera* found its most remarkable expression in the work of Giacomo Meyerbeer (1791–1864), whose first French opera, *Robert le Diable*, dates from 1831. Shortly before this work appeared two other examples had come from composers normally associated with very different styles of opera: Auber, whose *Masaniello* was produced in 1828, and Rossini, whose last opera, *William Tell*, appeared in 1829. But the honours for *Grand Opera* go to Meyerbeer, for it is in his works that the style can be seen at its most impressive and at its worst. His masterpiece is probably *Les Huguenots* (1836), but there is much to be said for *Le Prophète* (1845) and *L'Africaine*, produced posthumously in 1865.

The essence of a Meyerbeer opera is theatrical effect. He took historical events for his subject matter and treated them with all the respect for truth normally associated with Hollywood film epics. He loaded his operas with striking choruses, luscious melodies, brilliant orchestral effects, and decked them with strong romantic situations and splendid scenery. Unfortunately he seldom knew quite when to stop. If *Robert le Diable* caused a sensation with a

85

ballet of dead nuns, then there was nothing for it but that *Les Huguenots* must drag in the Massacre of St Bartholemew's. The audience was to be dazzled at all costs—there were to be impressive effects even if no real cause could be found to justify them. Yet he had considerable originality and worked at his operas with scrupulous care. They were enormously popular in their day and even now can be revived successfully when the right singers turn up. Historically he is of great importance, for his style influenced both Verdi and Wagner, not to mention a host of lesser men.

Alongside *Grand Opera* the lighter style of *Opéra-comique* developed in its own way, gradually taking over some of the technical features of serious opera. Eventually the only difference between the two styles was that the *Opéra-comique* used spoken dialogue instead of a sung recitative. In its classic phase French *Opéra-comique* is represented by Boieldieu (*La Dame Blanche*, 1825), Auber (*Fra Diavolo*, 1830), and Herold (*Zampa*, 1831). During the middle years of the century a slightly more frivolous style developed in the delightful art of Jacques Offenbach (1819–80), whose *Orphée aux Enfers* (1868), *La Belle Hélène* (1864) and *Les Contes d'Hoffmann* (1881) still hold the stage.

About the same time there also developed a form of opera that made use of spoken dialogue but was rather more serious than *Opéra-comique*. It deserves, perhaps, the special title of *Lyric Opera*; and it is best represented by Ambroise Thomas (1811–96) and Charles Gounod (1818–93), whose operas *Mignon* (1866) and *Faust* (1859) are, respectively, their finest works.

Only one other aspect of French opera need be mentioned—the work of that isolated figure, Hector Berlioz (1803–69). Despite the fact that his masterpiece, *Les*

Opera in the Nineteenth Century

Trojans, written during 1856–58, is, in all externals a *Grand Opera*, Berlioz had little in common with the Meyerbeers of his time. In spirit *Les Trojans* looks back to Gluck. It has a monumental, classic grandeur, plus a true romantic warmth and passion. In all essentials the music of *Les Trojans* is equal in dignity to Virgil's epic poem which provided Berlioz with his initial inspiration. The trappings may be those of nineteenth-century *Grand Opera*, but the spirit is that of ancient Greece. It is thus one of the great operatic masterpieces of all time.

National opera in Germany dates from the first performance of Weber's finest opera *Der Freischütz* (1821). Before this date the nearest approach to a specifically 'German' opera had been Mozart's *Die Zauberflöte*, but this, as we have seen, was a unique work that had no true successor. Carl Maria von Weber (1786–1826) may thus be regarded as the founder of German opera in general and German *Romantic Opera* in particular.

One of the characteristics of the Romantic Movement was its glorification of folk art (one more aspect of the rising tide of nationalism). In Germany we see this trend in such publications as the *Fairy Tales* of the brothers Grimm, which appeared between 1812 and 1815. Historical novels, fairy stories, legends and folk tales followed in great profusion and all combined to create a new kind of national mythology. Opera soon joined the general trend and one of the most successful and influential of its contributions was *Der Freischütz*.

Most of its elements were inherited from the eighteenth-century *Singspiel*—a pure heroine, a likeable but easily misled hero, evil deeds that rebound upon the villain, a background of merry peasants and a spine-chilling touch of the supernatural. What distinguishes Weber's treatment of these conventional ingredients is the conviction with which they are painted in music. The supernatural horrors really do chill the spine; the heroine's music has something of Beethoven's nobility; while the cheerful peasant music is irresistibly charming. In his own way Weber was able to repeat Mozart's feat of combining simple tunes and a sophisticated approach without spoiling either. Certain themes, those representing good and evil for example, are used throughout the work and thus give it an impressive sense of unity. Over and above everything else is his sumptuous orchestration, which heralds a new approach to the instruments whereby their tonal colour becomes an important means of creating atmospheric effects. Despite moments of great beauty and originality Weber's last two operas, *Euryanthe* (1823) and *Oberon* (1826), did not live up to the promise of *Der Freischütz* and his career was cut short before he could properly develop his enormous gifts. But the point had been made—German opera had discovered its identity.

For the moment, however, its progress hung fire. Weber's immediate successor, Heinrich Marschner (1795–1861), lacked his authority, though his supernatural operas *Der Vampyr* (1828) and *Hans Heiling* (1833) achieved a wide popularity. There is, perhaps, more lasting value in some of the lighter pieces written in the old *Singspiel* tradition: Lortzing's *Zar und Zimmerman* (1847), Nicolai's *Lustigen Weiber von Windsor* (1849), Flotow's *Martha* (1847) and Cornelius's *Der Barbier von Bagdad* (1858). But German opera still had some time to wait before finding its authentic voice in the triumphant uproar of Wagner's music. In the meantime it sank to a faint echo of Weber's promise.

Italian serious opera, which had successfully resisted

outside influence during the eighteenth century, finally began to take note of the changes that had begun to take place at the beginning of the nineteenth century. Ironically, the key figure in bringing about the change was a German, Simon Mayr (1763–1845) who spent most of his life in Italy. Mayr persuaded Italian audiences to forego the rigid patterns of serious opera and accept a more flexible style in which arias and recitative might be more varied, the chorus play a more important part, and, most important of all, in which the orchestra might be raised to something rather better than a mere banjo accompaniment. Gradually he set the pattern that was to be followed by Italian composers throughout the nineteenth century.

Opera buffa, on the other hand, was already more forward looking, and, continuing through the delightful works of Cimarosa (1749–1801), eventually reached a high-water mark in the music of Gioacchino Rossini (1792–1868). His career is without parallel in the history of opera. He produced his first important opera in 1810, when he was eighteen, and for nearly twenty years poured out a stream of works, sometimes at the rate of four a year. And then, after 1829, he wrote no more for the stage, preferring to fill out the odd corners of his life as a wealthy *bon-viveur* by composing little trifles to give pleasure to himself and his friends. Precisely why he refused to continue his spectacular career may never be known, but it is possible that he felt himself to belong more to the eighteenth century than the nineteenth. His last opera, *William Tell*, is in fact a fine example of French *Grand Opera*. Perhaps having proved he could rise to the new challenge he decided that it wasn't worth the trouble. His greatest contribution, however, is the string of *Opera buffa* masterpieces which culminated in *The Barber of Seville* (1816) and *Cenerentola*

(1817). His music is clear and deft, melodious and witty; singer's opera, but supported by skilful and often subtle orchestration. Nor should his ability to handle serious opera be forgotten. Works like *Tancredi* (1813) and *Otello* (1816) contain much that is beautiful and effective.

After Rossini's abdication the Italian *Opera buffa* suffered an almost complete eclipse and the last traces are to be found in Donizetti's *Don Pasquale* (1843). But Donizetti's general style has more in common with the sentimental romance of French *Lyric opera*. Like Rossini, Donizetti (1797–1848) had the gift of melody and was equally ready to use it. He produced some sixty-seven operas during the twenty-eight years of his working life, saturating them with catchy tunes and bright, uncomplicated harmonies. The subjects he chose are typical of the period: semi-historical melodrama (*Lucrezia Borgia*, 1833), romantic sentimentality (*Lucia di Lammermoor*, 1835) and so forth. All of them found a ready and appreciative audience.

His contemporary, Vincenzo Bellini (1801–35), though superficially like him in general manner, showed a more fastidious taste and it is in his operas that the art of *bel canto* found its purest expression. The finest of his eleven operas, *La Sonnambula* (1831), *Norma* (1831) and *I Puritani* (1835), are distinguished by melodies of great refinement and elegance, reminiscent, it has often been pointed out, of Chopin.

The art of Bellini, and to a lesser degree of Donizetti, concentrates the whole of the drama in the melodic line. The harmony and orchestra play only a small part; what matters is the vocal line and, of course, the singer.

Already, then, it is possible to see the beginnings of the two tendencies that were to mature during the second half of the nineteenth century in the music of Richard Wagner and Giuseppi Verdi. The German, on the one hand, laying emphasis on the orchestra until it all but overwhelms the voice; the Italian, on the other, all the while maintaining the supremacy of the vocal line. In between there lay a third way which takes from both extremes. It is this compromise that produced the most fruitful results for the opera of the twentieth century.

XI

Wagner and Verdi

THE history of opera in the second half of the nine-teenth century is dominated by the figures of Wagner and Verdi. Though they were very different in character they had one thing in common: their music echoed the hopes and aspirations of their fellow-countrymen. In a sense Wagner *is* nineteenth-century Germany, Verdi *is* nineteenth-century Italy—just as Shakespeare *is* the England of the first Elizabeth.

Richard Wagner was born in Leipzig on May 22nd, 1813. As a boy he was interested first in writing poetic tragedies modelled on Shakespeare, whom he greatly ad-mired; but his discovery of Beethoven's music changed the direction of his ambitions and he resolved to become a composer. Apart from a handful of lessons he was practic-ally self-taught. More important, perhaps, were his first appointments as a professional musician, for they put him into close contact with the operatic world and gave him a thorough grounding in the general repertory of the day. Inevitably his own first attempts at writing opera (*Die Feen*, 1833, and *Das Liebesverbot*, 1835) drew on current models for inspiration, and in them passages reminiscent of Weber, Donizetti and Auber turn up in curious juxtaposition with traces of Beethoven.

Wagner and Verdi

In 1837 he found employment at Riga and began work on *Rienzi*, a *Grand Opera* on the Meyerbeer pattern. But the Riga appointment did not last long and, with a pack of creditors on their heels, Wagner and his wife fled first to England and then to Paris where, in a nightmare of poverty and frustration, he finished both *Rienzi* and a new score, *The Flying Dutchman*. At last his fortunes changed. *Rienzi* was accepted for Dresden in 1842 and its success led to a production of *The Flying Dutchman* in the following year.

In *Rienzi* Wagner succeeded in his aim of writing a work that would appeal to the sort of audiences that applauded Meyerbeer. *The Flying Dutchman*, however, owes more to the German *Romantic Opera* of Weber and Marschner; not only in the supernatural basis of its plot, but in its musical make-up. What distinguishes it as being the beginning of a new and original style is the quality of the music. This demonstrates very clearly his ability to conjure up a dramatic situation in a few notes, his inclination to explore new harmonies, and foreshadows, in the clear-cut, Beethovenish nobility of its themes, the epic quality of his mature work.

These qualities are even more apparent in Wagner's next opera: *Tannhäuser* (1845). The harmony is bolder than ever, and now the orchestra has begun to play an important part in revealing the nature of the drama. Moreover, recitative passages have now begun to develop into that style of writing that can best be thought of as a cross between pure declamation and irregular melody. And, whether he knew it or not, he had also begun to use his dramatic works to express his own spiritual problems, turning them, as it were, into autobiography.

Both *The Flying Dutchman* and *Tannhauser* deal with lonely heroes whose souls are eventually redeemed by the

selfless love of a pure woman. In *Lohengrin* (1850), his
next work, the hero is not only isolated, but of divine
origin—a Wagner hugging his prophetic mission. And
that Wagner thought of himself as having a divine mission
is quite clear from the many ponderous writings in which,
from about 1851, he undertook the task of explaining himself and his music.

Lohengrin marked the end of Wagner's dependence on
elements of orthodox opera. A period of silence followed,
during which he thought deeply about the nature of his art
and revealed his findings in the long series of literary self-
justifications already mentioned. It was almost as if he
needed to convince himself that his version of the truth
was the only possible one before he could bring himself to
carry out his theories in musical practice. The masterpieces which then followed overlap each other in order of
composition, thus:

	Composed	Performed
Tristan und Isolde	1857–59	1865
Die Meistersinger	1861–67	1868
Der Ring des Niebelungen:		
1. Das Rheingold	1853–54	1869
2. Die Walküre	1854–56	1870
3. Siegfried	1854–71	1876
4. Götterdämmerung	1870–74	1876
Parsifal	1876–82	1882

Of these the most important, from an historical point
of view, is the cycle of four *Music Dramas* grouped under
the general title of *The Ring of the Niebelungs*. Wagner's
original intention had been to write only one drama on the
legend of Siegfried. When he began to write the libretto,
in 1848, he found that the story needed so much explanation that he was forced to write another drama as a pro-

logue. But that too needed explanation, and so on until the whole had become a cycle of four dramas, to be performed on four consecutive evenings. The entire cycle was composed over a period of twenty years.

It is important to recognize that the characters in *The Ring* are not men and women in the ordinary sense, but are more like symbols of the different aspects of Wagner's philosophy. The cycle presents, in the form of an elaborate and rather confusing myth, the workings of those eternal natural forces that govern the relationship between man and his gods, man and nature, man and society—this, at least, is what Wagner claimed. Music was thus no longer to be mere entertainment, but was now to deal with aspects of thought normally associated with religion and philosophy.

Wagner made clear his scorn for ordinary opera by dropping the word altogether and using instead the term *Music Drama*. By this he meant that poetry was to be on an equal footing with music, and both, together with drama, architecture and painting, were to be regarded as different but equally necessary parts of a total art-work. For Wagner dramatic expression involved all the arts on equal terms.

In practice this meant that the old conventions of Aria and Recitative were no longer valid. Wagner was ready to scrap them altogether and in their place substituted a continuous flow of music built up like a symphony from many different themes. These themes, or *Leitmotivs*, represented different aspects of the drama—a character or an idea, an object or an emotion. The audience is expected to learn the significance of each theme on its first appearance and from then on recognize its meaning whenever it returns. The themes may be modified during the course of the drama

95

and each change has its own dramatic meaning—for example, a bold theme representing the hero might be distorted if it became necessary to show that the hero had grown corrupt.

Wagner thus transferred the whole burden of dramatic expression into the orchestra and left the voices with nothing more exciting to do than sing the essential words in a sort of melodic recitative against the continuous orchestral background. The only practical disadvantage lay in the fact that music built on symphonic lines takes time to unfold and make its point. To allow for this Wagner was forced to spin out the vocal lines and distort the words; worse, the dramatic action was held up while the orchestra made its meaning clear. In consequence Wagner's *Music Dramas* are several times the length of normal operas and can, therefore, try the patience of the most sympathetic listener. Yet even this length had its compensations, for it gave the works a monumental vastness in keeping with the portentous message they were supposed to convey, and certainly drove out any suspicion that they were to be thought of as mere entertainment.

The adoption of a symphonic style forced Wagner to expand his orchestral forces far beyond the dimensions of the normal theatre orchestra. This, coupled with the virtuoso nature of his orchestral writing, made it difficult for ordinary opera houses to perform his works adequately. His solution to the problem was typical: if his work would not fit into existing conditions then new conditions must be created. Eventually even this grandiose dream became a reality. King Ludwig II of Bavaria took Wagner under his wealthy, if rather eccentric, wing and in 1876 the Wagner Festspielhaus was opened at Bayreuth.

Of Wagner's mature works probably *Tristan und Isolde*

is the most perfect (though many people would put in a claim for *Die Meistersinger* as a comic masterpiece). The story of *Tristan* presents none of the problems of interpretation that bedevil the *Ring* cycle—a man and a woman are forced to love one another by the workings of a destiny beyond their control; ultimately they can find fulfilment only in death. Hardly anything happens on the stage. The true drama is played out in the orchestra as it reveals the emotions of the chief characters. It is a drama of ideas rather than people and thus the music has the greatest possible freedom to develop on its own terms. Harmonically *Tristan* represents the highest point of Wagner's development. Diatonic harmony is replaced by chromaticism —the continual melting from one dissonance into another through endless modulations. The effect is to set up an atmosphere of yearning and restlessness very much in keeping with the nature of the drama. Add to this the purely sensuous effects of the luxurious harmony and rich orchestration and it is obvious that all the essential parts of the drama are present in the fabric of the music. Everything in *Tristan* reaches out to one end, and the effect is overwhelming.

It would be difficult to overstate the immense impact Wagner made upon the whole art of music. He raised it to an unparalleled height of expressiveness, but in doing so contrived to undermine its very foundations. His successors were left not only gasping at his achievement, but with the problem of piecing together a shattered tradition. Today, seventy years after his death, the pieces are still being fought over.

Everything about Wagner, from his personal life to his art, was violent, explosive and exaggerated. By comparison Verdi appears, at first sight, a pale, uninteresting figure. In his private life he was modest, clear-minded and respectable. He argued no obscure philosophy, and, though he became a hero to his fellow-countrymen, did not consider it his duty as an artist to act as a prophet. He behaved, in fact, like an honest craftsman. What distinguishes him is precisely that quality that gave Mozart his incomparable power: the ability to investigate human emotion in terms of music that has a lasting significance. In Giuseppi Verdi Italy found her supreme musical dramatist.

He was born in 1813, of the humblest peasant stock. His musical education began at the village organ and continued in the local brass band. Fortunately he later found sympathetic teachers and, with their encouragement to back his own tenacity of purpose, he was soon able to make good the gaps in his education. None the less it must be emphasized that when he first began to make his mark as an operatic composer his manner of expression was still rough and ready. But he continued to learn throughout his long career and ultimately became the acknowledged master of the Italian operatic style.

His natural gifts, however, were enormous: a sure instinct for the theatre, a deep understanding of human nature and the ability to express this in an unfailing stream of powerful melody. Even at his worst his music has an irresistible force and vitality, a passionate integrity that cuts through to the core of things with the fine ring of truth.

Verdi's first important success came in 1842 with the production of his third opera *Nabucco*. Overnight he became a national hero. His music was adopted by the patriotic movement that eventually freed Italy from Austrian domination. The operas that followed *Nabucco* during the next ten years all exploit situations that could be interpreted by the audience in terms of the political struggle, even though they hoodwinked the Austrian censor.

Verdi's music follows the conventions of the period, but has a vigour that makes his immediate predecessors, Donizetti and Bellini, seem very small beer. Although his powers of orchestration grew in subtlety over the years all the important effects in his operas are made through the voices. Unlike his German contemporary he clung to the human voice as the true means of expressing human emotion.

Maturity, already hinted at in *Macbeth* (1847), found its first expression in *Rigoletto* (1851). This work has a Mozartian quality in that it is a conversation opera with a greater number of duets than solos. The same can be said of *La Traviata* (1853), in which the orchestra began to play a greater part in the dramatic development and in which the music itself achieves a greater degree of subtlety and refinement than ever before.

One of the great influences on Verdi's work came from the Meyerbeer school of *Grand Opera*. This can be seen in the vast choruses and intensely dramatic *scenas* of such works as *Simon Boccanegra* (1857) and *Don Carlos* (1867). There is, however, a distinct advance in the art of organizing long scenes into a musical unity by means of appropriate orchestral motives. These never challenge the supremacy of the voice, but act as a subtle commentary on the dramatic action. Needless to say, the actual musical quality of Verdi's themes is far superior to anything in the usual run of *Grand Opera*.

The climax of Verdi's indebtedness to Meyerbeer came with *Aida* (1871) written to celebrate the opening of the Suez Canal. This work has everything the earlier master might have dreamed of: an exotic subject with unrivalled opportunities for spectacular effects, triumphal marches, ballets, vast choruses, and a story that runs the whole gamut of strong emotions. Verdi rose to the occasion magnificently, not only surpassing himself but surpassing the whole idea of *Grand Opera*. The score possesses a greater degree of unity than anything he had yet done, besides being infinitely more subtle. The set-piece arias and ensemble are still evident, but they are welded together in such a way as to grow inevitably out of the dramatic situation. Certain themes recur throughout the opera—not in the pedantic Wagnerian fashion, but to underline a dramatic point.

After *Aida* nothing new came from Verdi's pen for sixteen years. Then, in 1887, to the complete surprise of an unprepared world, he produced *Otello*.

Verdi's interest in Shakespeare found its first musical expression in *Macbeth* (1847), and it is not too fanciful to say that his admiration for the great dramatist may well have helped him to understand the nature of his own genius. Now, at the age of 70, he was completely equipped to tackle Shakespeare on equal terms. The result is a masterpiece. It is still possible to pick out the various 'numbers' in the work, for it is still in the tradition of Italian opera, but now the boundaries between aria and recitative are blurred over and the music flows majestically through each act. The drama still takes place in the voices, despite a vast increase in the importance of the orchestral commentary. Melodically and harmonically the work is infinitely more subtle and expressive than anything he had written before.

Yet he still had one more card up his sleeve. *Falstaff*, his last opera, was produced when he was eighty years old. It proved to be the climax of his life's work. The libretto was adapted by Arrigo Boito (the composer who had supplied the libretto for *Otello*) from Shakespeare's *Merry Wives of Windsor*. There is little that need be said about the music except that it belongs, as *Otello* does, to the short list of operatic masterpieces of all time. Arias and recitative melt into a continuous 'arioso' which varies in melodic intensity as the drama requires. The orchestration is delicate and extremely imaginative and provides a subtle commentary on the action. The traditions of Italian opera are preserved intact, but raised to a height that transforms them out of recognition.

Since there are no revolutions, no obscure philosophies, no mystical yearnings in Verdi's art it is easy to assume that he is somehow of lesser importance than Wagner. The fact is, of course, that the two men cannot properly be compared with one another. Wagner's greatness is his own—so too is Verdi's.

XII

Strauss and Puccini

IN comparison with the gigantic figures of Wagner and
Verdi the remainder of nineteenth-century opera is of
little interest, except in so far as the tide of nationalism encouraged substantial contributions from countries other
than Italy, France and Germany.

A new departure came from France with the production
of Bizet's finest opera, *Carmen* (1875). Although written
along the lines of *Opéra-comique*, with spoken dialogue,
set-piece arias, duets and choruses, the work broke fresh
ground by approaching a realistic subject in a realistic way.
The events in *Carmen* are so vivid that they might well
take place in real life.

Massenet's operas, on the other hand, have proved
rather less vital, though *Manon* (1884) has a graceful
lyricism that offsets the composer's rather sentimental approach to his subject. Both Massenet (1842–1912) and
Bizet (1862–75), however, pale in significance beside the
figure of Debussy (1862–1918), whose only opera *Pélléas
et Mélisande* was first produced in 1902. In a sense this
opera may be regarded as a deliberate and typically French
reaction against Wagner and his methods. Everything in
the opera is subordinate to the words: the vocal line is
narrow in range and only momentarily lyrical, the charac-

ters address each other in delicate recitative that follows the rhythms and natural rise and fall of the French language; the orchestra is similarly restrained. There are no passionate outbursts, the whole work is a study in muted colours and delicate understatement. However, the effect is astonishingly powerful and moving, for the music underlines the subtlest change of mood and atmosphere. Like *Les Trojans* of Berlioz, Debussy's masterpiece produced no school of its own and remains isolate and unique.

In Italy the anti-Wagner feeling produced rather more startling results in a school of 'realism', such as had been hinted at in Bizet's *Carmen*. This found its most concentrated expression in two short operas: *Cavalleria Rusticana* (1890), and *I Pagliacci* (1892). The composers, Mascagni (1863–1945) and Leoncavallo (1858–1919), were unable to repeat the success of these two works, and although both produced rather better music it always lacked the fire and violent passion of the two pieces that have carried their names down to posterity.

The true heirs of Wagner and Verdi were the two men whose operas dominated the early part of the twentieth century—Richard Strauss (1864–1949) and Giacomo Puccini (1858–1924). Both were brilliant craftsmen with a high degree of genuine originality, but both lacked the essential greatness of their illustrious predecessors. With all Wagner's technique at his command Strauss often chose to illustrate, in painful detail, sordid and sensational stories. Puccini, equally gifted, seldom rose higher than sentimentality and melodrama. Yet it must be admitted that within these limitations they were both fine musicians with a strong flair for the theatre, and that their operas have filled, and continue to fill, the opera houses of the world.

Richard Strauss achieved his first success as a composer

of Symphonic Poems and only turned to opera at the end of the nineteenth century. He scored his first great triumph with *Salome* (1905), an opera based on Oscar Wilde's sensational drama. Formally it is in the style of a Wagner *Music Drama*, with a complex symphonic background woven from striking themes. The orchestral texture is rich and brilliant, and the harmony reaches the extremes of dissonance. It is undoubtedly impressive. Yet the subject matter is distasteful, and Strauss's ability to underline each detail of the unpleasantness seems a two-edged gift. There is, too, a streak of the commonplace in his imagination that makes it impossible for him to create a really convincing climax to his horrors—in *Salome* the moment of supreme nastiness is lost in a banal waltz-tune. Much the same can be said of *Electra* (1909).

Strauss's third operatic masterpiece came as a complete and welcome contrast—even he may have felt that *Electra* had gone far enough. The work in question was *Der Rosenkavalier* (1911), a comedy of Viennese life in the eighteenth century. The music is no less complex than that of the earlier operas, but now the voice dominates the orchestra, tunes spill over in rich profusion and lush harmonies melt in continuous ecstasy. It is even possible to trace definite set-piece Arias and Ensembles.

This tendency to return to eighteenth-century principles is to be seen even more clearly in the beautiful music of *Ariadne auf Naxos* (1912). Strauss achieved less success with his later operas. His powers of invention fell off considerably after the First World War, leaving only a sad reminder of his former genius.

Puccini's sensationalism is, if anything, rather less repulsive. He at least seems to have been moved by the sufferings of his characters—Strauss, one suspects, rather enjoyed their miseries. But the range of character Puccini was content to explore is very narrow indeed and consequently all his operas bear a strong family likeness (mostly centring around pathetic little women who die for love). Musically he continued the pattern suggested by Verdi's last operas: a strong vocal line supported by a continuous orchestral background which is both an accompaniment to the voices and a commentary upon the drama. The orchestral background is not built up symphonically however, but pieced together from self-contained melodic fragments in the manner of a mosaic. Puccini's melodies, though powerful and of great sensuous beauty, are all marked by a peculiar melancholy which can only be described as self-pitying. He wrote only twelve operas, but half of these have become the mainstay of every opera house. There can be few people who have not heard and delighted in the music of *Manon Lescaut* (1893), *La Boheme* (1896), *Tosca* (1900), *Madame Butterfly* (1904) and *Gianni Schicci* (1918). His masterpiece is probably his last opera, *Turandot*, left unfinished at his death, but completed from sketches and eventually performed in 1926.

During the nineteenth century considerable progress was made towards establishing national opera in countries which had previously been content to import their entertainment from Italy. Czechoslovakia, for example, found its first voice in the music of Smetana's comic opera *The Bartered Bride* (1866). This melodious work is saturated with the spirit of Czech folksong and did much to inspire the Czechs with a feeling of national unity and thus helped them to throw off the yoke of Austrian domination. Smetana's work was ably followed by that of Dvořák, whose comic opera *The Devil and Kate* (1899) is no less important than his lyrical masterpiece *Rusalka* (1901).

An Outline of Operatic History

In more recent years Czech opera has risen to greater prominence in the music of Leos Janáček (1854–1928), whose style is based on a subtle translation of the rhythms of the Czech language. In Janáček's operas the vocal lines are almost entirely the melodic equivalent of speech, which rises at moments to passages of great lyrical intensity. *Jenufa* (1904), *Katya Kabanova* (1921) and *The Sly Vixen* (1924) are among the masterpieces of the twentieth century.

Native opera in Russia dates from the first performance of Glinka's *A Life for the Czar* (1836), though its real foundations were probably laid by his second and last opera, *Ruslan and Ludmilla*, produced six years later. Glinka's style, though reminiscent of German and Italian models, contains much that is characteristic of Russian folksong.

The leading Russian operatic composers of the later part of the century fall into two distinct groups: those who, like Tchaikovsky, modelled themselves on the operatic styles of Western Europe; and those who, like Borodin and Mussorgsky, were intent on creating an independent national style based on folksong. Tchaikovsky's two masterpieces, *Eugen Onegin* (1879) and *The Queen of Spades* (1890), are in the general style of *Romantic opera* and filled with graceful tunes, expressive harmonies and striking orchestration.

The composers of the nationalist school had little of Tchaikovsky's sheer technical mastery, but the great masterpiece of the movement, Mussorgsky's *Boris Gudunov* (written in various stages between 1868 and 1872), has a power and authority that cuts clean across convention. Apart from the music's grim strength the most original features of Mussorgsky's style are the massive choral scenes and the vivid manner in which he translates speech into music. *Boris Gudunov* is a work that burns with sincerity, a rough, ungainly and utterly convincing masterpiece.

Another aspect of Russian genius is displayed in the fairy-tale operas of Rimsky-Korsakov, which delight in colourful and rather exotic fantasy.

Though this is as far as a generalized sketch of operatic history can conveniently take us it would be wrong to regard opera as an exhausted art form. At the present moment it shows every sign of active, healthy life. Like music in general the styles it employs are nowadays rather mixed. Atonal operas, like Alban Berg's *Wozzeck* and Schönberg's *Moses and Aaron*, appear alongside works that hark back to the style of the eighteenth century, like Stravinsky's *The Rake's Progress*. Practitioners of debased Puccini, like Menotti, are the contemporaries of men, like Benjamin Britten, whose inspiration is in the highest tradition of opera.

It may even be that the solution to the present problems in music may be found through the opera house. In the past opera has exerted a profound influence on music— most of the great discoveries in harmony, orchestration and dramatic expression have been made in the opera house, and there is no reason why future benefits should not arise from the same source. For the operatic composer is placed in a very special position: he must use his fantasy to create convincing drama, but he must not be so fanciful that his ideas fail to get over the footlights. He is at once free to soar as high as he can, and is yet at the same time chained to the reality of the theatre. Nothing is more dead than a dead opera—nothing more stimulating than one that truly lives.

XIII

English Opera

THE history of English opera is short and singularly depressing. Although from time to time serious attempts have been made to establish a truly national operatic style either conditions have proved unfavourable or English composers too weak to take advantage of their opportunities. Only in very recent years has the prospect begun to look more hopeful.

It must be admitted, however, that the English temperament never seems to have taken kindly to the idea of opera. Plays with music have always been popular, but the notion that characters might express themselves entirely in song has always been regarded with suspicion. Such encouragement as opera has met with in this country has come mainly from the upper classes and has been directed, almost exclusively, to the support of whatever foreign import happens to have been fashionable at the time. Homegrown composers have met with little enthusiasm.

Possibly the very fact that the English theatre had already established itself before opera came into existence has had something to do with this curious situation. A glance at any Elizabethan play will show that music played an important part in the theatre. But even in the most music-conscious of these plays the rôle of music has been subordinate to that of poetry. Indeed, in the case of Shakespeare the sheer musicality of his poetry makes it quite unnecessary to call in music to heighten emotion (which is what happens in opera). Music is thus placed in a non-operatic position and is brought in either at moments when the characters can use it naturally (as a Song, or a Dance) or is kept as a means of showing that the character is in some way different from ordinary people (for example, Shakespeare's Witches and Fairies all sing; so do characters who have lost their reason, like Ophelia). The poetry in Shakespeare's dramas is so intense that it can express the highest emotions without the aid of music. A work like *The Tempest* is as operatic as any opera—but the arias are all poetry. In such circumstances the idea of opera came too late.

The English, however, were not entirely uninterested in 'recitative musick', as the new Italian invention came to be called; but the interest did not sweep the country and was confined, for the most part, to Court circles. There it found its main expression in the *Masques* that were so popular in the reigns of James I and Charles I. These were modelled on similar Italian and French entertainments and mixed dancing with poetry and song in a simple dramatic form, decked out with elaborate scenic effects. It is possible that the *Masques* might have led to the creation of a genuine operatic style, but the Civil War intruded and Court life and its frivolities were disbanded.

Paradoxically this turn of events led to the production of the first English 'opera'. Cromwell had closed the theatres, but seems to have had no objection to musical entertainments. Therefore, in 1656, the playwright William D'Avenant announced that he would perform an opera called *The Siege of Rhodes*. In fact all he did was to disguise a perfectly straightforward play by setting it in 'recitative musick'. Apart from the choruses that end each act there was only one Song in the whole piece. When the theatres were opened, with the restoration of the monarchy in 1660, D'Avenant quietly dropped his boasts about 'opera'.

By 1667 English taste had fixed upon the notion of a 'play, with music'—represented in this particular year by adaptation that D'Avenant and Dryden made of Shakespeare's *The Tempest*, with music by Pelham Humphrey, John Bannister and Matthew Locke. This, for the moment, came to be the substitute for real opera—a romantic play made more romantic by music added here and there.

The first entertainment that can properly be called an English opera is John Blow's *Venus and Adonis*, produced, probably in 1685, for the private entertainment of King Charles II. Everything about it is on a small scale, but it contains all the elements of a genuine opera—choruses, dances, songs and recitative, touches of humour and moments of passion. Blow called his work a *Masque*, despite the fact that it is sung throughout, like a true opera; but his description may account for the rather static plot, which indeed is masque-like. *Venus and Adonis* can hardly be counted as one of the great operatic masterpieces of the seventeenth century, but it has charm and vitality enough to make it still acceptable. More important, it seems to have served Purcell as a model for his great opera *Dido and Aeneas*.

Henry Purcell (1658–95) began his association with the theatre in 1680 but seems to have made little impression until about the year 1689 when he wrote a short entertainment for Josias Priest, a dancing-master who ran a school for young ladies in Chelsea. The entertainment took the form of an opera which could be performed by the pupils.

English Opera

The words were supplied by Nahum Tate, the poet laureate. *Dido and Aeneas*, the work in question, received its school performance and was promptly forgotten as a stage work until it was rescued by the Royal College of Music in 1895. Now it is universally recognized as a masterpiece.

Although Purcell's music owes something to French and Italian influence it is dominated by a forthright, vigorous quality that can only be called English. His tunes are lively and fresh, full of rhythmic vitality. When he wishes, as in Dido's tragic farewell to life at the end of the opera, he can reach the heights of dramatic passion. Equally impressive is his way with 'recitative musick', which translates the English language into music that expresses it both accurately and melodiously.

Unfortunately *Dido and Aeneas* was an isolated venture. Purcell was forced to turn his attention to the production of music for plays like *Dioclesian* (1690) and *The Indian Queen* (1695) which, though they make use of choruses, songs and dances, cannot rank as opera. The nearest he came to opera was in his collaboration with John Dryden over *King Arthur*, a play which incorporates a great deal of music. Dryden started from the assumption that human beings could not express themselves in song and thereupon proceeded to introduce into his story a variety of supernatural characters, for whom music would be the appropriate language. *King Arthur* is thus a 'semi-opera': a combination of music, drama and stage spectacle.

The next 'semi-opera' to come from Purcell's pen was an adaptation of Shakespeare's *Midsummer-night's Dream*, which was produced in 1692 under the title *The Fairy Queen*. It was so successful that a revival followed in 1693, with new songs added. Another adaptation from Shakespeare came in 1695, this time of *The Tempest*.

But 1695 was also the year of Purcell's death and with it all hope of founding a national style of opera vanished. Fashion inclined more and more to Italian opera and when, in 1710, Handel's operas appeared for the first time on the London stage the cause of English opera was lost. Had there been another English composer of Purcell's stature the story might have developed differently, but there was none and the Italian invasion went unchallenged.

In 1711 Joseph Addison, whose own opera *Rosamund* had failed badly, wrote, with understandable feeling:

At present our Notions of Musick are so very uncertain that we do not know what it is we like, only, in general, we are transported with anything that is not English: so if it be of foreign growth, let it be Italian, French or High-Dutch, it is the same thing. In short, our English Musick is quite rooted out, and nothing yet planted in its stead.

There were, however, some reactions and these first made themselves known through John Gay's *The Beggar's Opera*, which appeared in 1728. This work, a racy, up-to-date play about highwaymen and prostitutes, enlivened with simple songs and choruses all set to popular tunes of the day, took London by storm. It was everything the Italian opera was not—realistic, amusing, satirical, and belonging wholly to the people. Inevitably a flood of imitations followed.

Gradually the form developed and instead of borrowing tunes composers came to provide their own, though these remained simple in style. The most successful contributions to this new form, the *Ballad Opera*, came from: Thomas Arne (1710–78), Charles Dibdin (1745–1814), William Shield (1748–1829), and Stephen Storace (1763–96). Ballad operas were written well into the nineteenth century—Sir Henry Bishop's *Clari, the Maid of Milan*

(1823) is still remembered for the song 'Home, Sweet Home'.

Among the few attempts at serious opera must be mentioned Thomas Arne's *Artaxerxes* (1762), which was closely modelled on the Italian style and enjoyed a considerable success. However, it was an isolated effort and left no lasting mark.

Rather more fruitful was the blossoming of *Romantic Opera* in this country during the first half of the nineteenth century. Among the earliest examples are John Barnett's *The Mountain Sylph* (1834), Edward James Loder's *The Night Dancers* (1846) and Sir Julius Benedict's *The Lily of Killarney* (1862): all of which contain delightful music. More important, however, are the operas of the two Irish composers, Michael William Balfe (1808–70) and William Vincent Wallace (1812–65). Balfe began his spectacular career in 1835 with *The Siege of Rochelle*, a work in the style of French *Opéra-comique*. He wrote more than thirty operas and enjoyed a considerable reputation throughout Europe. His most popular work, *The Bohemian Girl* (1843), held the stage for many years. Wallace, though less prolific, achieved a similar success with *Maritana* (1845). Unfortunately the libretti of these works are more than usually absurd and the music, though tuneful enough, is not strong enough to make up the deficiences. Most of their operas have spoken dialogue, in the *Opéra-comique* tradition, and generally speaking skate over the problems of opera in too lighthearted a manner to count as significant contributions to the establishment of a native English style.

In the next generation further contributions came from Goring Thomas (*Esmerelda*, 1883), Frederick Cowen (*Thorgrim*, 1890) and Sir Charles Stanford (*Shamus O'brien*, 1896). Though their efforts and talents were of a more serious order they cannot be said to have made a more lasting impression than Balfe and Wallace, and they were certainly less successful with the general public of their own day. In the end it was comic opera that once more proved to be England's most fruitful source of a national operatic style—this time the series of brilliant operettas by Gilbert and Sullivan.

Sir Arthur Sullivan (1842–1900), who later proved his complete inability to write serious opera when he produced *Ivanhoe* in 1890, had a remarkable gift for sparkling tunes which superbly parodied the oddities of Italian and French opera. Brilliant orchestration, impeccable craftsmanship and the ability to probe out the subtleties of W. S. Gilbert's witty libretti, set his operettas head and shoulders above those of his contemporaries and firmly on a level with the best of Offenbach and Johann Strauss. The Gilbert and Sullivan triumphs include: *HMS Pinafore* (1878), *The Pirates of Penzance* (1880), *Iolanthe* (1882), *The Mikado* (1885) and *The Yeomen of the Guard* (1888).

It is ironic that at the very moment when English composers capable of tackling the problems of serious opera began to appear their chances of finding encouragement and performance in their own country began to decline. There were few opera houses outside London and these were served mostly by travelling companies capable only of limited productions. Now even these began to disappear. Some composers, like Frederick Delius (1882–1934) and Ethel Smyth (1858–1944), turned to the continent for performances. Delius's operatic masterpiece *A Village Romeo and Juliet* was first produced in Berlin in 1907; while Ethel Smyth's finest piece, *The Wreckers*, was first heard in 1906 at Leipzig. Both had to wait several years before being acknowledged in this country.

Thus it is hardly surprising to find another talented composer, Rutland Boughton (1878–1960), attempting to set up his own theatre at Glastonbury. His scheme was surprisingly successful in what it accomplished during the twelve years of its existence and deserves to be remembered as a pioneer experiment in the field of Music Festivals. His operas, which began heavily under the influence of Wagner, reached their maturity in a style based on folk-song. *The Immortal Hour*, the most successful of them, created a record for English opera when it ran for many months in London during 1922–23–24. But equally beautiful are *Bethlehem* (1915), *Alkestis* (1922) and *The Queen of Cornwall* (1924).

Vaughan Williams (1872–1959), also contented himself with semi-amateur performances for many years. His ballad opera *Hugh the Drover* was first performed by the Royal College of Music in 1924—ten years after it was completed! The College also performed what may well be his operatic masterpiece, *Riders to the Sea* (1937). It was not until 1951, when he was recognized as the leading English composer of the day, that any stage work of his had the honour of a completely professional first performance. The work in question, *The Pilgrim's Progress*, called by the composer a 'morality in music', shares with the best work of certain other English composers, like Boughton and Delius, a curious un-operatic quality—an inwardness of feeling—that places it apart from ordinary opera. Perhaps this does not make for worldly success, but it gives these works an individual beauty that cannot be dismissed.

Indeed, this theatrical reticence is noticeable in most English composers and it might be argued that the English temperament does not lend itself to the special art of opera, were it not for the work of Purcell and Britten. In the music of these two masters we have something that can stand comparison with the finest operatic composers of all time.

Benjamin Britten (b. 1913) began his operatic career immediately after the Second World War with *Peter Grimes*, which was produced by Sadler's Wells in 1945. This was followed by *The Rape of Lucretia* (1946), *Albert Herring* (1947), *Billy Budd* (1951), *Gloriana* (1953), *The Turn of the Screw* (1954), and *A Midsummer-night's Dream* (1960). In its superficial aspects Britten's operatic style ranges widely, drawing inspiration from Purcell and Verdi, among others. What is individual is his remarkable melodic gift which is capable of summing up a great variety of emotions in precise and unforgettable terms. His orchestration is brilliant and evocative, and his sense of theatre assured. His operas often deal with unusual subjects, though a basic preoccupation with the conflict between good and evil is common to them all. Few English composers since Purcell have had anything approaching Britten's sensitive understanding of the peculiarities of the English language; he sets words in a manner that is both startling and inevitable.

So far Britten is unique in this country, and almost unique in Europe, for his mastery of operatic problems. Certain other composers, notably Sir William Walton (*Troilus and Cressida*, 1953), Lennox Berkeley (*Nelson*, 1953), and Michael Tippett (*The Midsummer Marriage*, 1952; *King Priam*, 1962), show individual and valuable qualities, but none of them have Britten's easy mastery. Thus the future of English opera is closely bound up with Britten's development. Let us hope that, unlike Purcell, he will not be left without worthy successors.

Index

Index

Index